LANDLORDS' DUTIES AND TENANTS' RIGHTS

in Texas

Practicum Press

Practicum Press
Austin, Texas

Printed in the United States of America

ISBN 979-8-4092667-9-0

Acknowledgments

I would like to thank Amanda Peters and Steve Schumacher for their time and effort in reading the manuscript as well as adding valuable insights.

TABLE OF CONTENTS

CHAPTER 1

INTRODUCTION

THE RELATIONSHIP BETWEEN landlords and tenants is generally governed by the Texas Property Code and by various Texas court rulings. For example, Chapter 91 of the Texas Property Code contains provisions that are applicable to all landlords and tenants. Residential tenancies and commercial tenancies are covered by Chapters 92 and 93 of the Texas Property Code, respectively. This book is mainly focused on residential tenancies.

In conjunction, there are specific federal laws concerning anti-discrimination, military personnel, and credit reporting that affect residential and commercial tenancies.

Anti-Discrimination

Federal laws that are specifically related to anti-discrimination include Civil Rights Act, Americans with Disabilities Act and Fair Housing Act.

Civil Rights Act

The Civil Rights Act of 1968 (42 U.S.C. §§ 3601-3617) generally bars any policy that has a discriminatory effect. The 1988 Amendment to the Civil Rights Act of 1968 added provisions barring discrimination against handicapped persons and families with children. Basically, a landlord may not refuse to make reasonable accommodations in rules, policies, practices or services if necessary for a disabled person to use housing. A landlord must allow a disabled person to make modifications to a rented property to accommodate the disabled person's specific needs. However, the disabled person must remove the modifications and return the property to its original condition at the end of the lease.

Americans with Disabilities Act

Americans with Disabilities Act (ADA) of 1990 (42 U.S.C. § 12101) requires that reasonable accommodations must be made in commercial buildings so that people with disabilities can have access to those buildings.

When a commercial building is not accessible, it must be modified if access is reasonably achievable without undue burden or undue hardship.

Since the ADA applies to businesses, it is applicable to landlords and their commercial tenants. The only exemptions under the ADA are for religious organization and private clubs.

Fair Housing Act

Federal Fair Housing Amendments Act of 1988 along with the Texas Fair Housing Act (Chapter 301 of the Texas Property Code) prohibit discrimination by landlords regarding renting to a particular person based on race, color, national origin, religion, gender, familial status or disability. Familial status refers to whether or not a prospective tenant has minor children in a residential tenancy situation.

A landlord cannot take any of the following actions based on a person's race, color, national origin, religion, gender, familial status or disability:

a. refuse to rent housing;
b. refuse to negotiate for housing;
c. make housing unavailable;
d. set different terms, conditions or privileges for rental of a dwelling;
e. provide different housing services or facilities;

f. falsely deny that housing is available for inspection or rental; and

g. threaten, coerce, intimidate or interfere with anyone exercising a fair housing right.

It is also illegal to advertise or to make any statement that indicates a limitation or preference based on race, color, national origin, religion, gender, familial status, or disability.

A landlord can use any other factor to determine to whom the landlord wants to rent as long as that factor does not have the obvious effect of discriminating against one or more of the above-mentioned seven groups. For example, a landlord may use financial history, criminal history, previous rental history, and eviction records to determine whether the landlord wants to rent to a tenant.

Military Personnel

The Soldiers' and Sailors' Civil Relief Act of 1940 (50 U.S.C. §§ 530-534) was intended to lessen the financial hardship faced by military personnel and their families caused by active military service. Eligible military service persons who have executed leases before entering the service have unqualified right to terminate the leases when the military service persons give their landlord a written notice of termination after entering the service.

The Soldiers' and Sailors' Civil Relief Act also prohibits any person from knowingly seizing or detaining the tenant's property in an effort to claim rent after the lease terminates.

Credit Reporting

According to the Federal Fair Credit Report Act (15 U.S.C. § 1681 *et seq.*), a landlord who desires a credit report from an applicant as part of the rent application process must obtain the applicant's written permission to run the credit check. If the landlord declines to rent to the applicant based on the applicant's credit report, the landlord must inform the applicant in a "Notice of Adverse Action." The notice must contain the proscribed information and a toll-free telephone number or email address where the applicant may contact the credit reporting agency.

CHAPTER 2

RENTAL APPLICATION

THE RENTAL PROCESS typically begins with an applicant (*i.e.*, potential tenant) submitting a rental application.

Application Fee

Typically, an applicant is required to submit an *application fee* along with a rental application. An application fee, as defined by the Texas Property Code § 92.351, means a nonrefundable sum of money that is given to a landlord to offset the costs of screening an applicant for acceptance as a tenant. The screening commonly includes background and credit checks.

Application Deposit

A landlord can refuse to hold a property for an applicant without receiving an *application deposit* or hold deposit from the applicant. An application deposit, as defined by the Texas Property Code § 92.351, means a sum of money that is given to a landlord in connection with a rental application and that is refundable to an applicant if the applicant is rejected as a tenant. An application deposit is not considered a security deposit (to be explained in Chapter 4) because there is no lease agreement between parties at this point. The application deposit can be converted to a security deposit only after a rental lease has been signed.

An application deposit needs to be returned to an applicant after the applicant has been rejected. An applicant is considered rejected if not accepted by the seventh day after the submission of a rental application or payment of an application deposit (Texas Property Code § 92.352). However, Texas Property Code does not provide a specific deadline for the returning of the application deposit to an applicant after the applicant has been rejected.

Similarly, Texas Property Code does not specify what should happen to the application deposit if an applicant changes his/her mind. In general, whether or not a landlord can keep an application deposit after an applicant has changed his/her mind about leasing a property usually depends on the terms stated on a form agreement and the understanding between the two parties. For example, some form agreements state that if an applicant fails to sign the lease within three days after a landlord has approved the applicant, the landlord can keep the entire application deposit.

Notice of Eligibility Requirements

Along with the application form, a landlord must provide, in writing, a notice indicating the landlord's criteria for accepting or denying the application. The criteria may include the applicant's criminal history, previous rental history, current income, credit history, or failure to provide accurate or complete information on the application form (Texas Property Code § 92.3515(a)).

The applicant must sign an acknowledgment form indicating the notice was provided. If the form is not signed by the applicant, it is presumed that the notice was not provided to the applicant.

The notice may be part of the rental application if the notice is underlined or in bold print. The notice must include a statement substantively equivalent to the following:

Signing this acknowledgment indicates that you have had the opportunity to review the landlord's tenant selection criteria. The tenant selection criteria may include factors such as criminal history, credit history, current income, and rental history. If you do not meet the selection criteria, or if you provide inaccurate or incomplete information, your application may be rejected and your application fee will not be refunded.

CHAPTER 3

RENTAL AGREEMENT

OTHER THAN RELEVANT federal and state laws, the most important document that governs the landlord/tenant relationship is a rental agreement, commonly known as a lease, between a landlord and tenant.

Lease Requirements

A lease is any written or oral agreement between a landlord and tenant that establishes or modifies the terms, conditions, rules, or other provisions regarding the use and occupancy of a dwelling (Texas Property Code § 92.001). Dwelling is defined as one or more rooms rented as a permanent residence to one or more tenants.

The minimum requirements for a lease include:

> - names of landlord and tenant;
> - a description of the property being leased;
> - a statement indicating a lease is created;
> - a rental period covered by the lease;
> - rent amount;
> - payment terms; and
> - signatures by landlord and tenant (if in writing).

Although an oral lease can be legally binding, a written lease is preferable because the lease terms can be more easily proven in court.

Under a legal doctrine called the statute of frauds, any lease with a term longer than one year must be in writing and signed by both the landlord and tenant in order to be enforceable. In addition, a lease of over one year is not valid without two witnesses to a landlord's signature. However, if a tenant accepts the benefits of a lease, even if it is not properly witnessed, the tenant may be "estopped" from contesting the lease's validity.

After a lease has been signed by a landlord and tenant, the lease is legally binding on both the landlord and tenant. There is no Texas law allowing a rescission period for an executed lease.

Texas law requires a landlord to provide at least one residential tenant on a lease with a copy of the written lease within three days of execution, or within three days of a tenant's written request for a copy of the lease. Failure of a landlord to provide a copy of a lease to a tenant within the three requested days will prevent a landlord from enforcing the lease, except for non-payment of rent.

Statutory Obligations

While landlords and tenants are generally free to set the terms of a lease, certain obligations imposed on landlords and tenants by the State of Texas cannot be waived, and some of these obligations are listed under § 92.006 of the Texas Property Code. For example, a landlord's duties and a tenant's remedies relating to security deposits, security devices, and utility cutoffs cannot be waived. Similarly, a landlord's duty to install a smoke detector and a tenant's remedy for the landlord's failure to install one are not waivable.

Also, the maximum number of adult occupants in a leased residential dwelling is limited to no more than three times the number of bedrooms in the dwelling, unless the landlord is required by law to allow a higher occupancy (Texas Property Code § 92.010).

In addition, federal laws require a landlord to give a tenant a Lead Paint Disclosure form along with a pamphlet called Protect Your Family From Lead in Your Home if the rental property was built before 1978. This rule applies to both written and oral leases and to all rental properties except for efficiencies (*i.e.*, no bedroom) and those specifically for the elderly.

14

As part of the lead-based paint disclosure, a landlord has a duty to disclose any known information regarding lead-based paint or paint hazards. A landlord must also provide any records or reports related to lead-based paint to a tenant. A lease must include an attachment stating that the landlord has complied with all the legal requirements, and the attachment must be signed and dated by both the landlord and tenant.

Optional Provisions

Even though some provisions are not required for an agreement to qualify as a lease, it is a good idea to include them in a lease. The following are some examples of optional provisions that are helpful.

Form of payment

If a landlord desires to restrict the acceptable forms of payment, there must be a specific clause in the lease requiring tenants to pay by check, money order or other forms of payment; in the absence of such a clause, a landlord must accept payment in the form offered, including cash (Texas Property Code § 92.011). The landlord is also required to give the tenant a receipt for the rent payment and to maintain a record of the payments and payment dates in a record book.

Late fees

Late fee can be charged against a tenant when the rent is paid after the due date of the rent. However, according to Texas Property Code § 92.019, a landlord may not collect from a tenant a late fee for failing to pay any portion of the tenant's rent unless:

(1) a notice of the late fee is included in a written lease;

(2) the late fee is reasonable; and

(3) any portion of the tenant's rent has remained unpaid two full days after the date the rent was originally due.

Thus, provisions for late fees should be included in the lease. Returned check fees should also be included in the lease.

A late fee may include an initial fee and a daily fee for each day any portion of the tenant's rent continues to remain unpaid, and the combined fees are considered a single late fee.

Pets

A lease should contain a provision regarding whether or not pets will be allowed. If pets are allowed, the lease should also state the amount of the pet deposit or monthly pet fee.

Assistance and service animals are technically not considered as pets,

Chapter 121 of the Texas Human Resources Code requires landlords to rent to disabled persons who need assistance animals. Landlords cannot use a "no pets" rule to prohibit assistance animals, but a pet deposit can be charged against tenants requiring assistance animals.

Under the Americans with Disabilities Act (ADA), a service animal is defined as a dog that has been individually trained to do work or perform tasks for an individual with a disability. The tasks performed by the dog must be directly related to the person's disability.

Under § 121.002 (1) of the Texas Human Resources Code, an assistance animal or a service animal is defined as a dog that is specially trained or equipped to help a person with a disability and is actually used by a person with a disability.

Neither ADA nor Texas Human Resources Code covers emotional support animals (*i.e.*, animals that provide a sense of safety, companionship, and comfort to those with psychiatric or emotional disabilities or conditions) because emotional support animals are not specially trained to do particular types of work for their owners, even though they often have therapeutic benefits.

In lieu of pet fee, a landlord may be able to charge a security deposit and/or seek money from a tenant if there is any damage caused by the assistance animal, service animal, or emotional support animal to the home. Also, if there is a nuisance issue, a landlord has the right to try to remove the assistance animal, service animal, or emotional support animal through legal proceedings.

Landlord's right to enter

At times a landlord needs to enter a rental premise when a tenant is not present for the purpose of maintenance and/or repair. It is a good practice to include a provision in the lease granting the landlord a right to enter the rental premise.

Repair responsibilities

A landlord has a duty to repair a property condition that materially affects a tenant's health or safety, but the landlord is not required to repair or remedy a property condition that does not affect the tenant's health or safety (*see* Chapter 5). It is a good practice to list the person who will be responsible for the latter type of repairs.

Subletting

A tenant may not sublet unless a landlord agrees to such an arrangement (Texas Property Code § 91.005). The landlord may charge the tenant a subletting fee, and the amount of subletting fee should be stated in the lease.

Attorney's fee

This provision allows a landlord to collect attorney's fees from a tenant if the landlord prevails in court concerning a dispute between the landlord and tenant.

CHAPTER 4

SECURITY DEPOSIT

TEXAS LAW IS silent regarding security deposits for commercial leases. Texas Property Code § 92.101 *et. seq.* governs security deposits for residential leases. If a security deposit is required by a residential lease, a landlord may choose to offer a tenant an option to pay a fee in lieu of a security deposit (Texas Property Code § 92.111).

Amount

Texas does not have any law limiting the amount of security deposit a landlord may require. An amount equal to onemonth's rent is a typical amount for a security deposit.

Texas also does not have any law requiring in what type of account security deposits must be kept.

Refund

A landlord must refund a security deposit within thirty days after a tenant has moved out of a rental property (Texas Property Code § 92.103). However, a landlord need not provide the refund until a forwarding address has been given by a tenant in writing (Texas Property Code § 92.107).

A landlord may deduct any damages and charges under a lease from the security deposit, except for damages from ordinary wear and tear. If any of the security deposit is kept, a landlord must give a tenant a written description and itemized list of all deductions, and refund any balance of the security deposit. The description and itemized list are not required if the tenant owes rent when the tenant moves out, and the amount owed is not disputed (Texas Property Code § 92.104).

If a landlord fails to refund a security deposit, or to give a proper accounting of damages and charges within thirty days after a tenant has

21

moved out of a rental property, the landlord is presumed to have acted in bad faith. If the landlord violates this section, the landlord is liable for $100 plus three times the security deposit wrongfully withheld, and reasonable attorney's fees (Texas Property Code § 92.109).

If a tenant substitutes the security deposit for the last month's rent, the tenant can be sued by a landlord for three times the unpaid rent plus reasonable attorney's fees (Texas Property Code § 92.108).

If a rental property is sold or otherwise transferred, except for in a foreclosure, the new owner is liable to the tenant for the security deposit. The old owner is also liable until the new owner accepts responsibility for the security deposit in writing (Texas Property Code § 92.105).

If a tenant does not move in a rental property after paying a security deposit or rent, a landlord cannot not keep the money if the landlord or tenant gets a replacement tenant, who is satisfactory to the landlord and who moves in by the date the original lease begins. However, the landlord can keep either a cancellation fee previously agreed upon or actual expenses incurred in securing the replacement tenant.

Lease without security deposit

If a tenant is liable for damages and charges on surrender of the premise when a security deposit is not required by a residential lease, a landlord may notify the tenant in writing of the landlord's claim for damages and charges on or before the date the landlord reports the claim to a consumer reporting agency or third-party debt collector (Texas Property Code § 92.110).

Chapter 5

Maintenance

TEXAS PROPERTY CODE does not specify who is responsible for maintenance in non-residential rental properties. Thus, all the maintenance responsibilities must be spelled out in a commercial lease.

Duty to Repair

For residential rental properties, a landlord has a duty to repair a property condition that materially affects the physical health or safety of a tenant when the tenant, who is not delinquent in rent payments, gives the landlord notice of the condition. The tenant's notice must be in writing if the lease requires a written notice. As mentioned in Chapter 3, the landlord's duty to repair cannot be waived by the terms of a lease. However, a landlord is not required to repair or remedy a condition that does not affect a tenant's physical health or safety, such as a defective dishwasher, and those repairs are typically defined by the terms of a lease.

After the receipt of a notice to repair or remedy, a landlord is required to make a diligent effort to repair or remedy a condition within a reasonable time. There is a rebuttal presumption that seven days is a reasonable time. If the landlord has not made the necessary repairs, a tenant is required to give a second notice to repair. The tenant can skip the second notice if the first notice is a written notice sent by certified mail with return receipt requested.

If the landlord has not made the necessary repairs after a reasonable time, the tenant can exercise the following remedies:

1. make the repair and then deduct the repair cost from the rent up the greater of one month's rent or $500;

2. terminate the lease; or

3. sue the landlord.

If the tenant chooses to make the repair and deduct the cost, a written notice needs to be given to the landlord stating the intention to make self-repair. The landlord can prevent the tenant from making self-repairs by delivering an affidavit to the tenant (Texas Property Code § 92.0561). In the affidavit, the landlord needs to make a sworn statement concerning the reason for delay and state facts showing the landlord has made and is making diligent efforts to repair the problem, including dates, names, addresses and telephone numbers of repairmen, etc., contacted by the landlord (Texas Property Code § 92.0562).

After receiving such an affidavit, the tenant may not do any repairs:

a. for 15 days if the delay is caused by unavailability of a needed part; or

b. for 30 days if the delay is caused by a general labor or material shortage due to a natural disaster.

If the cause of the delay continues, the landlord may deliver subsequent affidavits up to six month, while the landlord must continue to use diligent efforts to complete the repairs.

If the tenant chooses to terminate the lease for the landlord's failure to make a repair, the tenant is entitled to a refund of rent from the date of termination or move out and a refund of security deposit (Texas Property Code § 92.056).

If the tenant chooses to sue the landlord for failure to make required repair, the tenant may recover one month's rent plus $500, actual damages, and attorney's fees.

Security Devices

Texas Property Code § 92.153 requires that security devices to be installed at the landlord's expense and without any specific request from tenants. In general, every rental property must be equipped with:

- a window latch on each exterior window;
- a doorknob lock or keyed dead bolt lock on each exterior door;
- a sliding door pin lock on each exterior sliding glass door;
- a sliding door handle latch or sliding door security bar on each exterior sliding glass door; and
- a keyless bolting device and a door viewer on each exterior door.

For French doors, one of the doors must meet the above-mentioned general requirements, and the other door must have bolts that go into the top and bottom of the doorjamb.

A keyed dead bolt or keyless bolting device must be installed at least thirtysix inches from the floor, and cannot be higher than forty-eight inches from the floor. The keyed dead bolt or keyless bolting device must have a strike plate screwed into the doorjamb or be installed into a door with a metal doorjamb. The bolt must have a throw of at least one inch. The sliding glass door pin lock or security bar must be no more than fortyeight inches from the floor. Additional technical specifications for the required security devices can be found in Texas Property Code § 92.154.

There are exceptions related to housing for senior citizens and the disabled. If the dwelling is part of a multi-unit complex in which the majority of tenants are over the age of 55 or have a mental or physical disability, and as part of a written lease or some other written agreement the landlord is expressly required or permitted to periodically check on the health and welfare of the tenant, then the unit does not have to have a keyless bolting device. If a property is rented to a tenant who is either over the age of 55 or has a mental or physical disability and has requested in writing (separate from the lease) that a keyless bolting device not be installed, then one is not required.

A landlord who knowingly deactivates or does not install a keyless bolting device and falsely claims that one of the exceptions applies is subject to the tenant remedies set forth in Texas Property Code § 92.164(a)(4).

Rekeying Locks

A landlord is required to rekey exterior locks operated by keys or cards no later than seven days after each change of tenant at the landlord's expense (Texas Property Code § 92.156). However, any subsequent rekeying or changing of security device at the request of a tenant shall be paid for by the tenant.

If a tenant requests a landlord to rekey, repair or replace a security device, the landlord must act within a reasonable time, presumed to be seven days (Texas Property Code § 92.161). However, if the landlord has been notified of an unauthorized entry in a multi-unit complex, or if a crime of personal violence has occurred in the multiunit complex within the months prior to the request, then the reasonable time period is reduced to seventytwo hours. The amount of time that is considered reasonable can be increased if the landlord, through no fault of his or her own, does not know of the tenant's request, if the materials or labor or utilities are unavailable, or if the delay is caused by circumstances beyond the control of the landlord.

If a landlord does not comply with the security device requirements, a list of remedies is available to a tenant under Texas Property Code § 92.164. The tenant's first option is to install or rekey the security device himself/herself and to deduct the cost of materials, labor, etc. from the next rent payment. The tenant's second option is to send a written request for compliance with the security device laws to the landlord. If the landlord does not comply by the third day after the receipt of the notice, then the tenant can terminate the lease. This second option is subject to some limitations found in Texas Property Code § 92.164. The tenant's third option is to sue the landlord for violating the laws on security devices. If the tenant has not given the landlord any written request for compliance, the tenant can ask for actual damages, court costs, and attorney's fees. If the tenant has given the landlord a written request for compliance, the court can order the landlord to bring the dwelling into compliance with the law, and the tenant can also recover actual damage, punitive damages, and a civil penalty of one month's rent plus $500, attorney's fees and court costs.

When the repair or replacement of a security device is caused by damage or misuse of the security device by a tenant or the tenant's guest, a landlord can require the tenant to pay for the cost if there is a provision in the lease authorizing the landlord to charge the tenant, and the provision is underlined in the lease.

A landlord can require the tenant to pay for the cost in advance when:

a. the lease authorizes such advance payment;

b. the landlord notifies the tenant within a reasonable time after the tenant makes the request that advance payment will be required; and

c. the tenant is more than thirty days delinquent in reimbursing the landlord for damages for a security device caused by the tenant.

The landlord can also require the tenant to pay in advance if the tenant has requested a repair or change to the same security device, including a request to rekey, within the previous thirty days.

Smoke Detectors

Each one-family or two-family dwelling constructed in Texas must have working smoke detectors installed in the dwelling in accordance with the smoke detector requirements of the building code in effect in the political subdivision in which the dwelling is located. (Health and Safety Code, Title 9, subtitle A, § 766.002(a)). Subchapter F of Chapter 92 of the Texas Property Code contains provisions related to smoke detectors in residential properties. In general, smoke detectors must be able to detect both visible and invisible products of combustion; have an alarm that is audible to the bedroom it serves; be powered by battery, alternating current or other power source (determined by local ordinance); be approved by Underwriters Laboratories, Inc., Factory Mutual Research Corporation or United States Testing Company, Inc.; and be in good working order.

Each bedroom must have its own smoke detector. When multiple bedrooms are served by a single corridor, smoke detectors must be placed outside the bedrooms, but near the bedrooms. If a bedroom is located above the living and cooking areas, then the smoke detector must be installed in the center of the ceiling directly above the top of the stairway. If the dwelling uses only one room for dining, living and sleep, then the smoke detector should be installed inside such room.

Smoke detectors must be placed either on the ceiling or the wall. If they are placed on the ceiling, they cannot be within six inches of the wall. If they are placed on the wall, they must be within six and twelve inches of the ceiling.

Landlord's obligation

At the beginning of each tenant's possession, the landlord has a duty to check smoke all smoke detectors on premise to ensure that they are in working order. The duty to check smoke detectors is satisfied when the landlord has either used the testing button or followed other test procedures recommended by the smoke detector manufacturer.

During an extension or renewal of a lease, the landlord does not have a duty to check smoke detectors unless the tenant gives the landlord notice that there is a malfunction, and requests the landlord to inspect or repair the smoke detector. After the tenant has made this request, the landlord needs to comply with the request within a reasonable time, presumed to be seven days. The exception to this obligation is when the damage to the smoke detector is caused by the tenant or a guest of the tenant. In those situations, the landlord does not have to act unless the tenant pays in advance for the reasonable repair or replacement costs.

If the landlord violates the laws related to smoke detectors, remedies available to tenants include seeking a court order directing the landlord to comply with the tenant's request, seeking a judgment against the landlord for damages suffered by the tenant because the landlord's violation, or terminating the lease (Texas Property Code § 92.260).

A landlord is not liable to a tenant if the tenant is not current on rent when the written notice is given or has not paid the costs in advance.

Tenant's obligations

A tenant is liable for damages to a landlord for removing a battery from a smoke detector without immediately replacing it with a working battery, or for knowingly disconnecting or intentionally damaging a smoke detector, causing it to malfunction. If the lease between the landlord and tenant contains a notice in underlined or boldfaced print warning the tenant not to disconnect or intentionally damage a smoke detector, or warning the tenant to replace a battery that has been removed from the smoke detector by the tenant, the landlord may be able to obtain a court order directing the tenant to comply with the landlord's notice, to pay a civil penalty of one month's rent plus $100, attorney's fees and court costs (Texas Property Code § 92.2611).

A landlord must give a tenant written notice in a separate document that the landlord intends to exercise his/her remedies if the tenant does not reconnect, repair or replace the smoke detector within seven days after being notified.

Carbon Monoxide Detectors

Texas State law does not require the installation of carbon monoxide (CO) detectors in rental properties. But in order to improve safety and reduce risks of carbon monoxide poisoning, some cities have enacted ordinances requiring a rental property within city limits to be outfitted by a CO detector when there is a gas or fuel-burning appliance (*e.g.*, gas stove, gas dryer, fireplace, gas-powered furnace, etc.) in the property, or when the living area is directly connected to a garage (*i.e.*, there is a door leading to garage from kitchen or through a utility room).

Local regulations vary based on the municipality, so it is important to check a website of a city/town in order to find out more information on whether the city/town has adopted the CO detector requirements.

The National Association of Fire Protection recommends that a CO alarm should be centrally located outside of each separate sleeping area in the immediate vicinity of the bedrooms.

For example, a CO detector should be installed near a bedroom if there is anything in the house that uses fuel or gas, as well as inside the bedroom if the room has or connects to a room that has fuel or gas. On the other hand, CO detectors should not be installed in garages, kitchens, furnace rooms, or in any extremely dusty, dirty or greasy areas.

Fire Extinguisher

A landlord does not have a duty to install fire extinguishers in dwelling units. But if a landlord has installed a 1A10BC residential fire extinguisher as defined by the National Fire Protection Association or other non-rechargeable fire extinguisher in accordance with a local ordinance or other law, the landlord has to inspect the fire extinguisher at the beginning of a tenant's possession, and within a reasonable time after receiving a written request by the tenant (Texas Property Code § 92.263).

The inspection must include checking to ensure the fire extinguisher is present, and checking to ensure the fire extinguisher gauge or pressure indicator indicates the correct pressure as recommended by the manufacturer of the fire extinguisher.

Pesticide Application

The Texas Structural Pest Control Act (Chapter 1951 of the Occupations Code) governs who may apply pesticides to apartment buildings. An apartment building owner must obtain pest control services from either a business with a structural pet control business license or an employee who is a licensed certified noncommercial applicator. Uncertified apartment building owners are prohibited from applying pesticides to an apartment building containing two or more dwelling units.

The Structural Pest Control Act provides certain exemptions. Unlicensed individuals may use pesticides to prevent, control or eliminate pest infestation on their own premises or on premises in which they own a partnership or joint venture interest. Also, people who use pest control chemicals available in retail stores for household application are exempt if the insecticide is used by the owner, employee or agent in space occupied by the building owner in a residential building, or used in a place that is vacant, unused and unoccupied.

Mildew and Mold

Many people confuse mildew with mold. Although mildew and mold are both fungi, and mildew can cause similar allergic reactions to that of mold, mildew is not as invasive or troublesome as mold. Mildew is much easier to eliminate, so it is less of a threat.

Differences between mildew and mold

Mildew is typically found in the surface of wet areas. Mildew looks grayish-white and may turn brown. It has a powdery texture with a foul odor.

Mold usually grows underneath the surface of anything that has gotten wet. Its texture can be fuzzy or slimy and has a musty smell. It appears as irregularly shaped spots that can have different colors such as blue, green, yellow, brown, gray, black, or white. Oftentimes, surfaces that are covered in mold begin to rot.

Effects of mildew and mold

Mold and mildew have different effects on the surfaces where they grow and the people who live in their vicinity. Mildew typically does not leave lasting damage to surfaces.

The effects of mold tend to be more serious. Mold can damage entire structures, and can result in considerable structural damage when left unattended for a long time. Depending on the strain of mold, prolonged exposure to mold may cause a variety of health problems such as allergic reactions (*e.g.*, sneezing, skin irritations, irritation of the eyes and throat, nasal congestion, etc.), respiratory problems (*e.g.*, difficulty breathing, coughing, pneumonia, asthma attacks), heart problems, migraines, inflammation and pain in the joints, dizziness, depression, and extreme fatigue. The mycotoxins produced by black mold are particularly harmful and may have severe long-term health effects, especially in children and individuals with weak immune systems.

Test mold and mildew

The easiest way to identify the kind of microorganisms in a dwelling is to drip a few drops of household bleach on the affected area and wait for about five minutes before inspecting the spot:

- if it has become lighter, it is mildew;

- if it remains dark, it is mold.

A more thorough mold evaluation and testing can be performed by a mold remediation company.

Clean mildew and mold

In order to clean mildew, all it typically needs is bleach, vinegar, or mildew cleaner and a good scrubbing brush. However, mold is not something that most people should be cleaning themselves. Mold removal is best left to professionals.

The safest and most efficient way to get rid of a mold problem is to call a mold remediation company.

Prevent mildew and mold

The best way to prevent mildew and mold is to keep all the areas dry and moisture free. In addition, maintain a humidity level of about 40-50% inside a house, have heating and cooling systems regularly inspected, keep air ducts clean, ensure good air circulation inside the house, fix any leaks in bathrooms, kitchen or other areas, etc.

CHAPTER 6

RETALIATION

SOME LANDLORDS MAY attempt to retaliate against their tenants as a way to "punish" them for exercising their legal rights. Provisions regarding retaliation against tenants by landlords are covered under Subchapter H of Chapter 92 of the Texas Property Code.

Prevent Landlord's Retaliation

In order to prevent landlord's retaliation against tenants, certain actions are not allowed to be taken by landlords against their tenants if their tenants, in good faith, exercise or attempt to exercise a right granted by the lease, municipal ordinance, state laws and/or federal laws. For example, within six months after the date of a tenant's action, a landlord cannot:

a. deprive the tenant of the use of the rental property;

b. decrease services to the tenant or increase rent; or

c. terminate the tenant's lease.

Filing an eviction proceeding against a tenant, within six months of the tenant's lawful action, is considered as retaliation against the tenant unless the tenant:

a. is delinquent on the rent;

b. has damaged the property;

c. threatens the personal safety of the landlord, the landlord's employees or another tenant;

d. has materially breached the lease; or

e. was held over in violation of the law.

Furthermore, the landlord cannot act in bad faith to materially interfere with the tenant's rights under the lease.

If a landlord retaliates against a tenant, the tenant can sue the landlord for a civil penalty of one month's rent plus $500, actual damages, court costs and attorney's fees.

Prevent Tenant's Retaliation

A tenant cannot retaliate against his/her landlord either. For example, a tenant does not have a right to withhold rent because a landlord fails to make repairs when the condition needing repair does not materially affect the tenant's health and safety. Otherwise, the landlord may file suit against the tenant for unpaid rent in this situation.

If a tenant files a retaliation compliant against a landlord in bad faith, the landlord can file a counterclaim against the tenant. The court can evict the tenant from the premise, as well as penalizing the tenant for one month's rent plus $500, actual damages, court costs and attorney's fees.

CHAPTER 7

COLLECTING UNPAID RENTS

SOMETIMES IT IS a difficult task for a landlord to collect unpaid rents from a tenant. But even if the tenant is delinquent with the rent, the landlord cannot remove from the rental property doors, windows, locks, doorknobs, or any other appliance (such as a refrigerator or stove) supplied by the landlord.

Exempt Property

Unless the property has been abandoned by a tenant, a landlord cannot take the tenant's *exempt* property under any other circumstance. The following types of property are considered exempt property:

a. clothing;
b. tools, equipment, and books of tenant's trade;
c. school books;
d. one automobile and one truck;
e. family portraits and pictures;
f. one couch, two living room chairs, one dining table and chairs;
g. all beds and bedding;
h. all kitchen furniture and utensils;
i. food and foodstuffs;
j. medicine and medical supplies;
k. anything the landlord knows belongs to someone else not living in the leased premises;
l. anything the landlord knows was purchased on a recorded credit arrangement that has not yet been paid for;
m. all agricultural implements; and
n. children's toys not used by adults.

Non-exempt Property

If a tenant fails to pay rent, a landlord may have a lien on all of the tenant's *non-exempt* property found in the rental property. The landlord can enforce a landlord's lien without taking any formal action in court only if it is explicitly mentioned in the lease, underlined or printed in bold print. The landlord's lien provides the landlord the right to peacefully take the tenant's non-exempt property and to sell it (after a proper time period and notice), to satisfy any outstanding rent. But the landlord cannot sell or dispose of the tenant's non-exempt property unless that right is also written in the lease.

When a tenant has abandoned the premise, a landlord is allowed to remove all the contents of the premises, without a specific lease provision.

There is no specific limit on the amount of the tenant's nonexempt property the landlord can take. Nevertheless, if the landlord takes property (valued at market prices) worth significantly more than the rent owed, the landlord may have to face a wrongful seizure suit. The landlord also cannot take tenant's non-exempt property for any other charge. In addition, government-owned or government-subsidized housing programs generally forbid landlord's liens.

The landlord must provide a tenant at least 30 days advance notice of the sale by certified and regular mail to the tenant's last known mailing address; indicate the time, date, and place of the sale; and provide an itemized account of the rent owed and the name of the person to contact for information. The tenant is allowed to redeem the property prior to the sale if the tenant pays the rent owed and the reasonable packing, moving and storage charges (if these charges are also specified in the lease).

The tenant is also allowed to go to the sale and purchase the tenant's own property. The landlord must take the money received from the sale and apply it to the rental account. The tenant is entitled to any remainder.

If a landlord willfully violates this law, a tenant may recover the greater of one month's rent or $500, return of any property not sold or proceeds from the sale, plus actual damages, and reasonable attorney's fees, less any past due rent.

Personal Property of Deceased Tenant

Unless a lease specifically provides otherwise during the term of the lease, a landlord can ask a tenant to provide the name, address, and telephone number of a person to contact upon the tenant's death, and a signed statement authorizing that person to access the tenant's unit in the presence of a landlord representative and remove the tenant's personal property. If the landlord does not request this information, the tenant can volunteer it at any time.

If a tenant is the sole occupant of the unit, a landlord has the right upon the tenant's death to remove and store the tenant's personal property. The landlord must turn over the tenant's property to the person designated by the tenant (or a person who is lawfully entitled to the tenant's property), but the landlord may require the person taking the tenant's property to sign an inventory. The landlord may dispose of the tenant's property 30 days after sending notice by certified mail to the tenant's designated person to pick up the tenant's property if the designated person does not contact the landlord and does not take possession of the tenant's property.

CHAPTER 8

LEASE TERMINATION

A LEASE CAN be terminated in several ways: by agreement between a landlord and tenant, allowances by Texas laws, end of the lease term, or breaking the lease by the landlord or tenant.

By Agreement

A landlord and a tenant can agree to change or completely terminate a lease at any time. An agreement between the landlord and tenant is the most preferable way to resolve many potential legal issues, especially when the tenant does not have a legally valid reason for moving before the end of the lease term.

Expiration of Lease Terms

The duration of the lease term is typically specified in a lease. After the lease term expires, the landlord-tenant relationship usually continues on a month-to-month basis, unless one of the parties indicates otherwise. Therefore, when the lease term is about to expire, the party wishing to terminate the lease on the expiration date must provide a notice of termination, as commonly required by the lease.

A 30-day notice is typically required to terminate a lease, preferably in writing. However, if a tenants pay rent more than once a month and the lease does not specify when the notice to terminate must be provided, it is sufficient to provide a termination notice equal to the interval between rental payments. For example, if a tenant pays rent weekly, the tenant or landlord needs to provide only one week's notice in order to terminate the tenancy.

Unless otherwise specified in a lease, a 30day notice to terminate can provide for termination on any day of the month, as long as the date of termination is at least one month from the date of the notice. If the notice terminates the tenancy on a day that does not correspond to the end of the month or the beginning of a rent paying period, a tenant needs only pay for rent up to the date of termination.

A tenant in the Housing Choice Voucher Rental Assistance Program (formerly known as Section 8 housing), government-owned or government-subsidized housing often has an additional protection concerning a lease renewal. For example, some government programs may require a landlord to have a good cause (which can be defined in a lease) if the landlord does not want to renew the lease or to terminate a month-to-month lease.

Allowances by Texas Laws

Texas law allows a tenant to terminate a lease prematurely under certain situations. For example, Texas Property Code § 92.016 allows tenants to terminate their leases following family violence. In addition, Texas Property Code § 92.0161 allows tenants to terminate their leases if the tenants or members of their families are victims of sexual offenses or stalking. Also, Texas Property Code § 92.017 allows military personnel to terminate their leases without penalty if they are transferred by the military or deployed for more than 90 days.

Whether a tenant can avoid liability for unpaid rent and other sums due before terminating a lease depends on the wording of the lease. If the lease contains the following language or its equivalent:

```
Tenants  may  have  special  statutory  rights  to
terminate  the  lease  early  in  certain  situations
involving family violence or a military deployment
or transfer,
```

the tenant cannot avoid any delinquent payments (Texas Property Code § 92.016(f) and § 92.017(g)). Similarly, if the lease contains the following language or its equivalent:

```
Tenants   may   have   special   statutory   rights   to
terminate   the   lease   early   in   certain   situations
involving sexual offenses or stalking,
```

the tenant cannot avoid any delinquent payments (Texas Property Code § 92.0161(g).

Breaking the Lease

Early termination

If a tenant chooses to break a lease but does not have a legal excuse for early termination, the tenant can be held liable for the remaining rental payments under the lease. The tenant can also be liable for damages to the property, and also reasonable cleaning fees when authorized by the lease. If the tenant moves out early and the tenant's security deposit is not enough to cover these charges, the landlord may pursue any actions to collect the funds, including the reporting of these charges to credit agencies when collection efforts are unsuccessful.

A tenant may find a replacement tenant as long as the landlord finds the replacement tenant acceptable. However, the landlord can charge the tenant a reasonable *reletting fee* for having to prepare the dwelling for reletting and for having to redo paperwork. The reletting fee must be a fair amount to cover actual expenses.

If a replacement tenant cannot be found, a landlord can charge the tenant only for the total rent owed under the rest of the lease but not for any reletting fee or other termination fee.

Lease term violations

If a tenant violates a provision of a lease, a landlord may seek to terminate the lease. Failing to pay rent, severely disturbing neighbors, and committing serious crimes on the property are all fair grounds for terminating a lease. Ultimately, the lease terms dictate whether or not the landlord can terminate the lease due to a particular violation. If a tenant violates a provision of the lease, a landlord may claim that the lease has been terminated, but the landlord usually intends to terminate the tenant's right of possession, but not the tenant's other obligations of the lease agreement (such as to pay rent).

A tenant in the Housing Choice Voucher Rental Assistance Program, government-owned housing or government-subsidized housing must commit a serious violation of the terms of a lease before a landlord can terminate the lease.

Even if a landlord terminates a lease (or the tenant's right to possession), the tenant still has the right to dispute the landlord's decision and stay in the rental property while seeking a judgment from a court. The landlord cannot physically remove the tenant from the premises unless an eviction suit has been properly filed and a final judgment and writ of possession have been issued against the tenant.

New owner

If a landlord sells or transfers the property to a new owner, the new owner is obligated to honor a tenant's lease and any other agreement the tenant made with the landlord. However, if the property is foreclosed on by a creditor, such as a bank, the creditor is not obligated to honor the lease (or other agreement), but the creditor must provide the tenants at least 30 days written notice to vacate as long as the tenants are current on their rent. Tenants are considered current on their rent if, during the month of the foreclosure sale, the tenants pay rent for that month to the landlord before receiving any notice that a foreclosure sale is scheduled, or the tenants pay rent for that month to the purchaser no later than the fifth day after the date of the receipt of a written notice of the name and address of the purchaser that requests payment.

52

CHAPTER 9

EVICTIONS

EVICTIONS ARE LEGAL means for removing people from premises when they no longer have a right of possession. For example, a landlord may choose to evict a tenant from a rental property by filing an eviction suit if the tenant fails to pay rent and/or refuses to vacate the rental property after the end of a lease period.

A forcible entry and detainer (FED) occurs when an unauthorized person enters another person's property without legal authority or by force, and refuses to surrender possession on demand (Texas Property Code § 24.001). On the other hand, a forcible detainer occurs when a person refuses to surrender possession of a property on demand (Texas Property Code § 24.002). Unlike FED, the person's entry in a forcible detainer situation does not have to be unlawful. Thus, most eviction proceedings initiated by landlords are forcible detainers, not FED, because the tenants' initial entry is usually lawful.

Eviction Suits

Even if a landlord has grounds with which to evict a tenant, the landlord must perform all of the following steps before the tenant can be legally evicted. A landlord may not remove a tenant from a rental property without a final order from a Justice of the Peace court.

Step 1:   Providing a Notice

The eviction process begins with a landlord giving a written notice to a tenant who is either in default under a lease or is holding over after the end of the lease term. The tenant is allowed to have at least three days' notice under Texas Property Code § 24.005 (or a different notice period under a written lease) to vacate the premises before the filing of a suit for eviction.

The notice to vacate should include the date by which the tenant must vacate the premise and should inform the tenant that a suit for eviction will be filed if the tenant does not vacate by the deadline. The notice should include a demand for possession of the premise, and it may include a demand for the tenant to pay any unpaid rent if applicable. The notice can be delivered to the tenant in person or by mail (Texas Property Code § 24.005(f)).

A tenant in Housing Choice Voucher Rental Assistance Program, government-owned housing or government-subsidized housing is usually entitled to longer notice periods, as well as an administrative hearing (known as a grievance hearing) before any of the eviction procedures can begin, unless the allegations include a drug offense or violent criminal behavior.

Step 2: Filing a Compliant

If the tenant remains on the property after the deadline in the notice has lapsed, the next step for the landlord is to file a written compliant with a Justice of the Peace court in the precinct in which the rental property is located. The complaint must state the specific reason the landlord has for terminating the tenant's right to possession. The landlord may also ask the court to award delinquent rent.

The landlord can recover attorney's fees from the tenant if the lease provides for attorney's fees, or if the landlord sent to the tenant at least 10 days before the date the eviction suit is filed via certified mail, return receipt requested or registered mail a notice to vacate that demanded that the tenant vacates before the 11th day after the date of the receipt of the notice, and warned the tenant about the possibility of having to pay attorney's fees (Texas Property Code § 24.006).

On the other hand, the tenant may recover attorney's fee from the landlord if the tenant successfully defends the eviction suit. Either prevailing party may recover all court costs.

Step 3:   Serving the Tenant

After the compliant has been properly filed, the court will serve the tenant with an official notice and a copy of the court papers advising the tenant of the date and time that the tenant must either appear in court or file an answer (or response) to the eviction suit.   A Justice of the Peace may simply set a trial date for the eviction case, usually within six to ten days, or require the tenant to answer the eviction suit either orally or in writing by a deadline at which time the tenant will be notified of a trial date.   If the tenant does not answer the eviction suit on or before the deadline, the tenant will lose the eviction suit by default.

The landlord has an option to file a possession bond for immediate possession.   If the landlord does so, the court papers will explain that the landlord may take possession of the premises six days from the date that the tenant has been served with the bond papers unless the tenant asks for a trial within the sixday period.   If the landlord has filed a possession bond and the tenant does not ask for a trial within the six-day period, the tenant will lose possession of the premises.

Step 4:   Appearing in Court

The landlord and the tenant must appear on the date set for trial in the Justice of the Peace court to present evidence.   The trial date is usually held between 6 and 10 days of receiving the court papers, or, if the tenant is required to answer the lawsuit, a few days after the tenant has submitted an answer to the court.

Both the landlord and tenant have the right to present their side of the case, including witnesses, receipts, cancelled checks, photographs, and any other evidence they deem to support their position.   The tenant may request a jury trial by paying an additional fee within five days of receiving the eviction papers.

Step 5:   Executing a Court Order

If the Justice of the Peace (or jury) finds that the tenant should be evicted, the Justice of the Peace will issue a judgment against the tenant, and, if the tenant does not appeal that judgment in five days, the landlord can request the Justice of the Peace to issue a writ of possession that allows a constable or sheriff to physically evict the tenant.   The writ of possession cannot be issued until the sixth day (counting weekends and holidays) after the Justice of the Peace signs the judgment (Texas Property Code § 24.0054(d)).

After a writ of possession has been issued, the tenant will be given 24hours notice that a constable or sheriff will supervise the removal of all persons and property from the premise.   However, the peace officers cannot execute a writ of possession if it is raining, sleeting or snowing.   Also, writs of possession are typically not executed on weekends or holidays because constables and sheriffs usually do not work on weekends or holidays.

A landlord may allow a tenant to stay in the premise even after the tenant has lost an eviction suit.   For example, a landlord may allow a tenant to stay if the tenant pays back rent and court costs before the six days are up.

Appeal an Eviction Decision

Filing Deadline

The party that loses an eviction suit in a Justice of the Peace court may appeal the decision and seek for a new trial in a County Court. The party wishing to appeal has five days after the Justice of the Peace signs the judgment to file an appeal with the Justice of the Peace court (Texas Property Code § 24.0052).

Bond Requirement

To appeal an eviction decision at the County Court, a tenant must either put up a bond or file a pauper's affidavit of inability to pay the bond. If it is the tenant who is appealing, the Justice of the Peace will commonly set the bond at two to three times the amount of the rent. A bond must be signed by the tenant and two others who have real estate in Texas (that no one lives on) or other sufficient assets (*e.g.*, savings accounts and/or stocks). The bond guarantees that the other party's costs for the appeal will be paid in case the tenant loses. A tenant can also deposit cash with the court in the place of a bond. The appealing party must also pay court costs for filing the appeal in the County Court.

If the tenant wins in the County Court, the tenant will receive the bond back and will be entitled to the court costs from the landlord. If the tenant loses, the landlord will be able to apply for some of the bond money, depending on the costs for obtaining possession and any lost rent.

If a tenant has a low income, very little money, and limited personal property, the tenant can appeal by filing a pauper's affidavit instead of posting a bond and paying court costs. A pauper's affidavit is a document, signed by the tenant, swearing that the tenant does not have enough money to make bond or pay costs. The Justice of the Peace court must make available to the tenant an affidavit that the tenant may use that meets the requirements for a pauper's affidavit (including, for example, name, the amount of spouse's various forms of income, the amount of available cash in checking and savings accounts, the property owned by the tenant, the tenant debts and monthly expenses, and the number and age of dependents of the tenant). The document must be notarized and filed with the Justice of the Peace court on or before the fifth day after the Justice of the Peace makes a decision. A landlord can contest the affidavit and force the tenant, at a financial hearing with the Justice of the Peace, to prove inability to pay. If the tenant loses this financial hearing, the tenant has five days to either post a regular bond with the Justice of the Peace court, as described above, or appeal this decision to the County Court.

If the tenant appeals the decision of the Justice of the Peace to deny the pauper's affidavit, the County Court will set a hearing to consider the tenant's evidence that the tenant cannot afford the bond. If the County Court does not approve the pauper's affidavit, the tenant can remain in possession of the premises only if the tenant files an appeal bond within five days of the County Court judge's decision.

Written Answer

If the appeal papers are properly filed, the tenant can stay in the premises during the appeal. However, if the tenant has filed a pauper's affidavit, as described above, and the landlord has claimed the tenant had violated the lease for non-payment of rent, the tenant must deposit the rent stated in the judgment (and notice) by the date stated in the notice from the Justice of the Peace, but not later than five days after the date the tenant filed the pauper's affidavit. Then, the tenant must continue to deposit monthly rental payments with the court wherever the case is, but usually the County Court, within five days of the due date under the lease until the trial date.

If a portion of the rent is payable by a government agency (*e.g.,* public housing, subsidized housing or a Housing Choice Voucher Rental Assistance Program rental voucher), the Justice of the Peace should determine and note in the judgment the portion to be paid by the government and the portion to be paid by the tenant. If the judge does not correctly determine these amounts, within five days of the court's judgment, the tenant must contest in writing the amount incorrectly determined by the court. If the tenant fails to make these monthly rental payments to the court, the County Court, after a hearing, may issue a writ of possession to have the tenant removed from the residence pending trial, and the tenant may be responsible for the landlord's reasonable attorney's fees in filing a motion regarding the tenant's failure to pay rent to the court.

No matter who appeals the case, a tenant must also file a written answer either in the Justice of the Peace court or in the County Court within eight days of the case being assigned to a County Court. If an answer is not filed, the tenant can lose the eviction case without having a trial.

CHAPTER 10

COMMON AND PUBLIC NUISANCES

THE STATUTES THAT deal with common and public nuisances at a multi-unit residential property are found in Chapter 125 of the Civil Practices and Remedies Code instead of the Texas Property Code.

Definitions

A multi-unit residential property is any improved real property with at least three dwelling units, including an apartment building or condominium. It does not include a single-family home, a duplex or a property where each dwelling unit is occupied by an owner.

A common nuisance exists when one or more of the following activities occur regularly on the premises:

- reckless discharge of a firearm as defined by § 42.01 of the Texas Penal Code;

- engaging in organized criminal activity as a member of a combination as defined by § 71.02 of the Texas Penal Code;

- delivery, possession, manufacture, or use of a controlled substance in violation of Chapter 481 of the Health and Safety Code;

- gambling, gambling promotion, or communication of gambling information as prohibited by Chapter 47 of the Texas Penal Code;

- prostitution, compelling prostitution, promotion of prostitution, or aggravated promotion of prostitution as prohibited by Chapter 43 of the Texas Penal Code;

- commercial manufacture, commercial distribution, or commercial exhibition of obscene material as prohibited by § 43.21 of the Texas Penal Code;

- aggravated assault as described by § 22.02 of the Texas Penal Code;

- sexual assault and aggravated sexual assault as described by § 22.011 and § 22.021, respectively, of the Texas Penal Code;

- robbery and aggravated robbery as described by § 29.02 and § 22.03, respectively, of the Texas Penal Code;

- unlawfully carrying a weapon as described by § 46.02 of the Texas Penal Code;

- murder and capital murder as described by § 19.02 and § 19.03, respectively, of the Texas Penal Code;

- continuous sexual abuse of young child or children as described by § 21.02 of the Texas Penal Code;

- massage therapy or other massage services in violation of Chapter 455 of the Texas Occupations Code;

- employing a minor at a sexually oriented business as defined by § 243.002 of the Local Government Code;

- trafficking of persons as described by § 20A.02 of the Texas Penal Code;

- sexual conduct or performance by a child as described by § 43.25 of the Texas Penal Code; or

- employment harmful to a child as described by § 43.251 of Texas Penal Code.

A public nuisance includes a combination or criminal street gang that continuously or regularly associates in gang activities. The habitual use of a place by a combination or criminal street gang for engaging in gang activity is also considered as a public nuisance.

Causes of Actions

A plaintiff may sue a person who maintains, owns, uses or is a party to the use of a place for the purposes constituting a common or public nuisance under § 125.001 *et seq.* of the Civil Practices and Remedies Code. The plaintiff may bring an action *in rem* if the property is being maintained or used as a common nuisance.

The person who maintains and tolerates the public or common nuisance may not introduce evidence of calling law enforcement or emergency assistance to abate the activities or posting signs prohibiting those activities as a defense.

If a court determines that a common or public nuisance exists at a multi-unit residential property, the court, on its own initiative or on the motion of a plaintiff, may order the appointment of a receiver to manage the property or render any other order allowed by law to abate the nuisance. The court can determine the management duties of the receiver, the receiver's fees, the method of payment and the payment periods. However, the appointment cannot exceed one year.

TEXAS PROPERTY CODE

Chapter 91: Provisions Generally Applicable to Landlords and Tenants

§ 91.001   Notice for Terminating Certain Tenancies
(a) A monthly tenancy or a tenancy from month to month may be terminated by the tenant or the landlord giving notice of termination to the other.
(b) If a notice of termination is given under Subsection (a) and if the rent-paying period is at least one month, the tenancy terminates on whichever of the following days is the later:
(1) the day given in the notice for termination; or
(2) one month after the day on which the notice is given.
(c) If a notice of termination is given under Subsection (a) and if the rent-paying period is less than a month, the tenancy terminates on whichever of the following days is the later:
(1) the day given in the notice for termination; or
(2) the day following the expiration of the period beginning on the day on which notice is given and extending for a number of days equal to the number of days in the rent-paying period.
(d) If a tenancy terminates on a day that does not correspond to the beginning or end of a rent-paying period, the tenant is liable for rent only up to the date of termination.
(e) Subsections (a), (b), (c), and (d) do not apply if:
(1) a landlord and a tenant have agreed in an instrument signed by both parties on a different period of notice to terminate the tenancy or that no notice is required; or
(2) there is a breach of contract recognized by law.

§ 92.002 Application
This chapter applies only to the relationship between landlords and tenants of residential rental property.

§ 91.003 Termination of Lease Because of Public Indecency Conviction
(a) A landlord may terminate a lease executed or renewed after June 15, 1981, if:
(1) the tenant or occupant of the leasehold uses the property for an activity for which the tenant or occupant or for which an agent or employee of

the tenant or occupant is convicted under Chapter 43, Penal Code, as amended; and

(2) the convicted person has exhausted or abandoned all avenues of direct appeal from the conviction.

(b) The fee owner or an intermediate lessor terminates the lease by giving written notice of termination to the tenant or occupant within six months after the right to terminate arises under this section. The right to possess the property reverts to the landlord on the 10th day after the date the notice is given.

(c) This section applies regardless of a term of the lease to the contrary.

§ 91.004 Landlord's Breach of Lease; Lien

(a) If the landlord of a tenant who is not in default under a lease fails to comply in any respect with the lease agreement, the landlord is liable to the tenant for damages resulting from the failure.

(b) To secure payment of the damages, the tenant has a lien on the landlord's nonexempt property in the tenant's possession and on the rent due to the landlord under the lease.

§ 91.005 Subletting Prohibited

During the term of a lease, the tenant may not rent the leasehold to any other person without the prior consent of the landlord.

§ 91.006 Landlord's Duty to Mitigate Damages

(a) A landlord has a duty to mitigate damages if a tenant abandons the leased premises in violation of the lease.

(b) A provision of a lease that purports to waive a right or to exempt a landlord from a liability or duty under this section is void.

Chapter 92: Residential Tenancies

SUBCHAPTER A: GENERAL PROVISIONS

§ 92.001 Definitions
Except as otherwise provided by this chapter, in this chapter:
(1) "Dwelling" means one or more rooms rented for use as a permanent residence under a single lease to one or more tenants.
(2) "Landlord" means the owner, lessor, or sublessor of a dwelling, but does not include a manager or agent of the landlord unless the manager or agent purports to be the owner, lessor, or sublessor in an oral or written lease.
(3) "Lease" means any written or oral agreement between a landlord and tenant that establishes or modifies the terms, conditions, rules, or other provisions regarding the use and occupancy of a dwelling.
(4) "Normal wear and tear" means deterioration that results from the intended use of a dwelling, including, for the purposes of Subchapters B and D, breakage or malfunction due to age or deteriorated condition, but the term does not include deterioration that results from negligence, carelessness, accident, or abuse of the premises, equipment, or chattels by the tenant, by a member of the tenant's household, or by a guest or invitee of the tenant.
(5) "Premises" means a tenant's rental unit, any area or facility the lease authorizes the tenant to use, and the appurtenances, grounds, and facilities held out for the use of tenants generally.
(6) "Tenant" means a person who is authorized by a lease to occupy a dwelling to the exclusion of others and, for the purposes of Subchapters D, E, and F, who is obligated under the lease to pay rent.

§ 92.002 Application
This chapter applies only to the relationship between landlords and tenants of residential rental property.

§ 92.003 Landlord's Agent for Service of Process
(a) In a lawsuit by a tenant under either a written or oral lease for a dwelling or in a suit to enforce a legal obligation of the owner as landlord of the dwelling, the owner's agent for service of process is determined according to this section.

(b) If written notice of the name and business street address of the company that manages the dwelling has been given to the tenant, the management company is the owner's sole agent for service of process.

(c) If Subsection (b) does not apply, the owner's management company, on-premise manager, or rent collector serving the dwelling is the owner's authorized agent for service of process unless the owner's name and business street address have been furnished in writing to the tenant.

§ 92.004 Harassment

A party who files or prosecutes a suit under Subchapter B, D, E, or F in bad faith or for purposes of harassment is liable to the defendant for one month's rent plus $100 and for attorney's fees.

§ 92.005 Attorney's fees

(a) A party who prevails in a suit brought under this subchapter or Subchapter B, E, or F   may recover the party's costs of court and reasonable attorney's fees in relation to work reasonably expended.

(b) This section does not authorize a recovery of attorney's fees in an action brought under Subchapter E or F for damages that relate to or arise from property damage, personal injury, or a criminal act.

§ 92.006 Waiver or expansion of duties and remedies

(a) A landlord's duty or a tenant's remedy concerning security deposits, security devices, the landlord's disclosure of ownership and management, or utility cutoffs, as provided by Subchapter C, D, E, or G, respectively, may not be waived. A landlord's duty to install a smoke alarm under Subchapter F may not be waived, nor may a tenant waive a remedy for the landlord's non-installation or waive the tenant's limited right of installation and removal. The landlord's duty of inspection and repair of smoke alarms under Subchapter F may be waived only by written agreement.

(b) A landlord's duties and the tenant's remedies concerning security devices, the landlord's disclosure of ownership and management, or smoke alarms, as provided by Subchapter D, E, or F, respectively, may be enlarged only by specific written agreement.

(c) A landlord's duties and the tenant's remedies under Subchapter B, which covers conditions materially affecting the physical health or safety of the ordinary tenant, may not be waived except as provided in Subsections (d), (e), and (f) of this section.

(d) A landlord and a tenant may agree for the tenant to repair or remedy, at the landlord's expense, any condition covered by Subchapter B.

(e) A landlord and a tenant may agree for the tenant to repair or remedy, at the tenant's expense, any condition covered by Subchapter B if all of the following conditions are met:

(1) at the beginning of the lease term the landlord owns only one rental dwelling;

(2) at the beginning of the lease term the dwelling is free from any condition which would materially affect the physical health or safety of an ordinary tenant;

(3) at the beginning of the lease term the landlord has no reason to believe that any condition described in Subdivision (2) of this subsection is likely to occur or recur during the tenant's lease term or during a renewal or extension; and

(4)(A) the lease is in writing;

(B) the agreement for repairs by the tenant is either underlined or printed in boldface in the lease or in a separate written addendum;

(C) the agreement is specific and clear; and

(D) the agreement is made knowingly, voluntarily, and for consideration.

(f) A landlord and tenant may agree that, except for those conditions caused by the negligence of the landlord, the tenant has the duty to pay for repair of the following conditions that may occur during the lease term or a renewal or extension:

(1) damage from wastewater stoppages caused by foreign or improper objects in lines that exclusively serve the tenant's dwelling;

(2) damage to doors, windows, or screens; and

(3) damage from windows or doors left open.

This subsection shall not affect the landlord's duty under Subchapter B to repair or remedy, at the landlord's expense, wastewater stoppages or backups caused by deterioration, breakage, roots, ground conditions, faulty construction, or malfunctioning equipment. A landlord and tenant may agree to the provisions of this subsection only if the agreement meets the requirements of Subdivision (4) of Subsection (e) of this section.

(g) A tenant's right to vacate a dwelling and avoid liability under § 92.016 or § 92.017 may not be waived by a tenant or a landlord, except as provided by those sections.

(h) A tenant's right to a jury trial in an action brought under this chapter may not be waived in a lease or other written agreement.

§ 92.007 Venue

Venue for an action under this chapter is governed by § 15.0115, Civil Practice and Remedies Code.

§ 92.008 Interruption of utilities

(a) A landlord or a landlord's agent may not interrupt or cause the interruption of utility service paid for directly to the utility company by a tenant unless the interruption results from bona fide repairs, construction, or an emergency.

(b) Except as provided by this section, a landlord may not interrupt or cause the interruption of water, wastewater, gas, or electric service furnished to a tenant by the landlord as an incident of the tenancy or by other agreement unless the interruption results from bona fide repairs, construction, or an emergency.

(c) Repealed

(d) Repealed

(e) Repealed

(f) If a landlord or a landlord's agent violates this section, the tenant may:

(1) either recover possession of the premises or terminate the lease; and

(2) in addition to other remedies available under law, recover from the landlord an amount equal to the sum of the tenant's actual damages, one month's rent plus $1,000, reasonable attorney's fees, and court costs, less any delinquent rents or other sums for which the tenant is liable to the landlord.

(g) A provision of a lease that purports to waive a right or to exempt a party from a liability or duty under this section is void.

(h) Subject to Subsections (i), (j), (k), (m), and (o), a landlord who submeters electricity or allocates or prorates nonsubmetered master metered electricity may interrupt or cause the interruption of electric service for nonpayment by the tenant of an electric bill issued to the tenant if:

(1) the landlord's right to interrupt electric service is provided by a written lease entered into by the tenant;

(2) the tenant's electric bill is not paid on or before the 12th day after the date the electric bill is issued;

(3) advance written notice of the proposed interruption is delivered to the tenant by mail or hand delivery separately from any other written content that:

(A) prominently displays the words "electricity termination notice" or similar language underlined or in bold;

(B) includes:

(i) the date on which the electric service will be interrupted;

(ii) a location where the tenant may go during the landlord's normal business hours to make arrangements to pay the bill to avoid interruption of electric service;

(iii) the amount that must be paid to avoid interruption of electric service;

(iv) a statement providing that when the tenant makes a payment to avoid interruption of electric service, the landlord may not apply that payment to rent or other amounts owed under the lease;

(v) a statement providing that the landlord may not evict a tenant for failure to pay an electric bill when the landlord has interrupted the tenant's electric service unless the tenant fails to pay for the electric service after the electric service has been interrupted for at least two days, not including weekends or state or federal holidays; and

(vi) a description of the tenant's rights under Subsection (j) to avoid interruption of electric service if the interruption will cause a person residing in the tenant's dwelling to become seriously ill or more seriously ill; and

(C) is delivered not earlier than the first day after the bill is past due or later than the fifth day before the interruption date stated in the notice; and

(4) the landlord, at the same time the service is interrupted, hand delivers or places on the tenant's front door a written notice that:

(A) prominently displays the words "electricity termination notice" or similar language underlined or in bold; and

(B) includes:

(i) the date the electric service has been interrupted;

(ii) a location where the tenant may go during the landlord's normal business hours to make arrangements to pay the bill to reestablish interrupted electric service;

(iii) the amount that must be paid to reestablish electric service;

(iv) a statement providing that when the tenant makes a payment to reestablish electric service, a landlord may not apply that payment to rent or other amounts owed under the lease;

(v) a statement providing that the landlord may not evict a tenant for failure to pay an electric bill when the landlord has interrupted the tenant's electric service unless the tenant fails to pay for the electric service after the electric service has been interrupted for at least two days, not including weekends or state or federal holidays; and

(vi) a description of the tenant's rights under Subsection (j) to avoid interruption of electric service if the interruption will cause a person residing in the tenant's dwelling to become seriously ill or more seriously ill.

(i) Unless a dangerous condition exists or the tenant requests disconnection, a landlord may not interrupt or cause the interruption of electric service under Subsection (h) on a day:

(1) on which the landlord or a representative of the landlord is not available to collect electric bill payments and reestablish electric service;

(2) that immediately precedes a day described by Subdivision (1); or

(3) on which:

(A) the previous day's highest temperature did not exceed 32 degrees Fahrenheit and the temperature is predicted to remain at or below that level for the next 24 hours according to the nearest National Weather Service reports; or

(B) the National Weather Service issues a heat advisory for a county in which the premises is located or has issued such an advisory on one of the two preceding days.

(j) A landlord may not interrupt or cause the interruption of electric service under Subsection (h) of a tenant who, before the interruption date specified in the notice required by Subsection (h)(3), has:

(1) established that the interruption will cause a person residing in the tenant's dwelling to become seriously ill or more seriously ill by having a physician, nurse, nurse practitioner, or other similar licensed health care practitioner attending to the person who is or may become ill provide a written statement to the landlord or a representative of the landlord stating that the person will become seriously ill or more seriously ill if the electric service is interrupted; and

(2) entered into a deferred payment plan that complies with Subsection (l).

(k) If a tenant has established, in accordance with Subsection (j), the circumstances necessary to avoid electric service interruption under that subsection, the landlord may not interrupt or cause the interruption of the tenant's electric service under Subsection (h) before:

(1) the 63rd day after the date those circumstances are established; or

(2) an earlier date agreed to by the landlord and the tenant.

(l) A deferred payment plan for the purposes of this section must be in writing. The deferred payment plan must allow the tenant to pay the outstanding electric bill in installments that extend beyond the due date of the next electric bill and must provide that the delinquent amount may be paid in equal installments over a period equal to at least three electric service billing cycles.

(m) A landlord may not interrupt or cause the interruption of electric service under Subsection (h) to a tenant who receives energy assistance for a billing period during which the landlord receives a pledge, letter of intent, purchase order, or other notification that the energy assistance provider is forwarding sufficient payment to continue the electric service.

(n) If a delinquent electric bill is paid, or a deferred payment plan is entered into, during normal business hours, the landlord shall reconnect the tenant's electric service within two hours of payment or entry into the deferred payment plan.

(o) A landlord may not interrupt or cause the interruption of electric service under Subsection (h) for any of the following reasons:

(1) a delinquency in payment for electric service furnished to a previous tenant;

(2) failure to pay non-electric bills, rent, or other fees;

(3) failure to pay electric bills that are six or more months delinquent; or

(4) failure to pay an electric bill disputed by the tenant, unless the landlord has conducted an investigation as required by the particular case and reported the results in writing to the tenant.

(p) A landlord who provides notice in accordance with Subsection (h) may not apply a payment made by a tenant to avoid interruption of electric service or reestablish electric service to rent or any other amounts owed under the lease.

(q) The landlord may not evict a tenant for failure to pay an electric bill when the landlord has interrupted the tenant's electric service under Subsection (h) unless the tenant fails to pay for the electric service after the electric service has been interrupted for at least two days, not including weekends or state or federal holidays.

(r) Subject to this subsection, a reconnection fee may be applied if electric service to the tenant is disconnected for nonpayment of bills under Subsection (h). The reconnection fee must be computed based on the average cost to the landlord for the expenses associated with the reconnection, but may not exceed $10. A reconnection fee may not be applied unless agreed to by the tenant in a written lease that states the exact dollar amount of the reconnection fee. A fee may not be applied to a deferred payment plan entered into under this section.

§ 92.0081 Removal of property and exclusion of residential tenant
(a) A landlord may not remove a door, window, or attic hatchway cover or a lock, latch, hinge, hinge pin, doorknob, or other mechanism connected to a door, window, or attic hatchway cover from premises leased to a tenant or remove furniture, fixtures, or appliances furnished by the landlord from premises leased to a tenant unless the landlord removes the item for a bona fide repair or replacement. If a landlord removes any of the items listed in this subsection for a bona fide repair or replacement, the repair or replacement must be promptly performed.
(b) A landlord may not intentionally prevent a tenant from entering the leased premises except by judicial process unless the exclusion results from:
(1) bona fide repairs, construction, or an emergency;
(2) removing the contents of premises abandoned by a tenant; or
(3) changing the door locks on the door to the tenant's individual unit of a tenant who is delinquent in paying at least part of the rent.
(c) If a landlord or a landlord's agent changes the door lock of a tenant who is delinquent in paying rent, the landlord or the landlord's agent must place a written notice on the tenant's front door stating:
(1) an on-site location where the tenant may go 24 hours a day to obtain the new key or a telephone number that is answered 24 hours a day that the tenant may call to have a key delivered within two hours after calling the number;
(2) the fact that the landlord must provide the new key to the tenant at any hour, regardless of whether or not the tenant pays any of the delinquent rent; and
(3) the amount of rent and other charges for which the tenant is delinquent.

(d) A landlord may not intentionally prevent a tenant from entering the leased premises under Subsection (b)(3) unless:

(1) the landlord's right to change the locks because of a tenant's failure to timely pay rent is placed in the lease;

(2) the tenant is delinquent in paying all or part of the rent; and

(3) the landlord has locally mailed not later than the fifth calendar day before the date on which the door locks are changed or hand-delivered to the tenant or posted on the inside of the main entry door of the tenant's dwelling not later than the third calendar day before the date on which the door locks are changed a written notice stating:

(A) the earliest date that the landlord proposes to change the door locks;

(B) the amount of rent the tenant must pay to prevent changing of the door locks;

(C) the name and street address of the individual to whom, or the location of the on-site management office at which, the delinquent rent may be discussed or paid during the landlord's normal business hours; and

(D) in underlined or bold print, the tenant's right to receive a key to the new lock at any hour, regardless of whether the tenant pays the delinquent rent.

(e) A landlord may not change the locks on the door of a tenant's dwelling under Subsection (b)(3) on a day, or on a day immediately before a day, on which the landlord or other designated individual is not available, or on which any on-site management office is not open, for the tenant to tender the delinquent rent.

(e-1) A landlord who changes the locks or otherwise prevents a tenant from entering the tenant's individual rental unit may not change the locks or otherwise prevent a tenant from entering a common area of residential rental property.

(f) A landlord who intentionally prevents a tenant from entering the tenant's dwelling under Subsection (b)(3) must provide the tenant with a key to the changed lock on the dwelling without regard to whether the tenant pays the delinquent rent.

(g) If a landlord arrives at the dwelling in a timely manner in response to a tenant's telephone call to the number contained in the notice as described by Subsection (c)(1) and the tenant is not present to receive the key to the changed lock, the landlord shall leave a notice on the front door of the dwelling stating the time the landlord arrived with the key and the street address to which the tenant may go to obtain the key during the landlord's normal office hours.

(h) If a landlord violates this section, the tenant may:

(1) either recover possession of the premises or terminate the lease; and

(2) recover from the landlord a civil penalty of one month's rent plus $1,000, actual damages, court costs, and reasonable attorney's fees in an action to recover property damages, actual expenses, or civil penalties, less any delinquent rent or other sums for which the tenant is liable to the landlord.

(i) If a landlord violates Subsection (f), the tenant may recover, in addition to the remedies provided by Subsection (h), an additional civil penalty of one month's rent.

(j) A provision of a lease that purports to waive a right or to exempt a party from a liability or duty under this section is void.

(k) A landlord may not change the locks on the door of a tenant's dwelling under Subsection (b)(3):

(1) when the tenant or any other legal occupant is in the dwelling; or

(2) more than once during a rental payment period.

(l) This section does not affect the ability of a landlord to pursue other available remedies, including the remedies provided by Chapter 24.

§ 92.009 Residential tenant's right of reentry after unlawful lockout

(a) If a landlord has locked a tenant out of leased premises in violation of § 92.0081, the tenant may recover possession of the premises as provided by this section.

(b) The tenant must file with the justice court in the precinct in which the rental premises are located a sworn complaint for reentry, specifying the facts of the alleged unlawful lockout by the landlord or the landlord's agent. The tenant must also state orally under oath to the justice the facts of the alleged unlawful lockout.

(c) If the tenant has complied with Subsection (b) and if the justice reasonably believes an unlawful lockout has likely occurred, the justice may issue, ex parte, a writ of reentry that entitles the tenant to immediate and temporary possession of the premises, pending a final hearing on the tenant's sworn complaint for reentry.

(d) The writ of reentry must be served on either the landlord or the landlord's management company, on-premises manager, or rent collector in the same manner as a writ of possession in a forcible detainer action.   A sheriff or constable may use reasonable force in executing a writ of reentry under this section.

(e) The landlord is entitled to a hearing on the tenant's sworn complaint for reentry. The writ of reentry must notify the landlord of the right to a hearing. The hearing shall be held not earlier than the first day and not later than the seventh day after the date the landlord requests a hearing.

(f) If the landlord fails to request a hearing on the tenant's sworn complaint for reentry before the eighth day after the date of service of the writ of reentry on the landlord under Subsection (d), a judgment for court costs may be rendered against the landlord.

(g) A party may appeal from the court's judgment at the hearing on the sworn complaint for reentry in the same manner as a party may appeal a judgment in a forcible detainer suit.

(h) If a writ of possession is issued, it supersedes a writ of reentry.

(i) If the landlord or the person on whom a writ of reentry is served fails to immediately comply with the writ or later disobeys the writ, the failure is grounds for contempt of court against the landlord or the person on whom the writ was served, under § 21.002, Government Code. If the writ is disobeyed, the tenant or the tenant's attorney may file in the court in which the reentry action is pending an affidavit stating the name of the person who has disobeyed the writ and describing the acts or omissions constituting the disobedience. On receipt of an affidavit, the justice shall issue a show cause order, directing the person to appear on a designated date and show cause why he should not be adjudged in contempt of court. If the justice finds, after considering the evidence at the hearing, that the person has directly or indirectly disobeyed the writ, the justice may commit the person to jail without bail until the person purges himself of the contempt in a manner and form as the justice may direct. If the person disobeyed the writ before receiving the show cause order but has complied with the writ after receiving the order, the justice may find the person in contempt and assess punishment under § 21.002(c), Government Code.

(j) This section does not affect a tenant's right to pursue a separate cause of action under § 92.0081.

(k) If a tenant in bad faith files a sworn complaint for reentry resulting in a writ of reentry being served on the landlord or landlord's agent, the landlord may in a separate cause of action recover from the tenant an amount equal to actual damages, one month's rent or $500, whichever is greater, reasonable attorney's fees, and costs of court, less any sums for which the landlord is liable to the tenant.

(l) The fee for filing a sworn complaint for reentry is the same as that for filing a civil action in justice court. The fee for service of a writ of reentry is the same as that for service of a writ of possession. The fee for service of a show cause order is the same as that for service of a civil citation. The justice may defer payment of the tenant's filing fees and service costs for the sworn complaint for reentry and writ of reentry. Court costs may be waived only if the tenant executes a pauper's affidavit.

(m) This section does not affect the rights of a landlord or tenant in a forcible detainer or forcible entry and detainer action.

§ 92.0091 Residential tenant's right of restoration after unlawful utility disconnection

(a) If a landlord has interrupted utility service in violation of § 92.008, the tenant may obtain relief as provided by this section.

(b) The tenant must file with the justice court in the precinct in which the rental premises are located a sworn complaint specifying the facts of the alleged unlawful utility disconnection by the landlord or the landlord's agent. The tenant must also state orally under oath to the justice the facts of the alleged unlawful utility disconnection.

(c) If the tenant has complied with Subsection (b) and if the justice reasonably believes an unlawful utility disconnection has likely occurred, the justice may issue, ex parte, a writ of restoration of utility service that entitles the tenant to immediate and temporary restoration of the disconnected utility service, pending a final hearing on the tenant's sworn complaint.

(d) The writ of restoration of utility service must be served on either the landlord or the landlord's management company, on-premises manager, or rent collector in the same manner as a writ of possession in a forcible detainer suit.

(e) The landlord is entitled to a hearing on the tenant's sworn complaint for restoration of utility service. The writ of restoration of utility service must notify the landlord of the right to a hearing. The hearing shall be held not earlier than the first day and not later than the seventh day after the date the landlord requests a hearing.

(f) If the landlord fails to request a hearing on the tenant's sworn complaint for restoration of utility service before the eighth day after the date of service of the writ of restoration of utility service on the landlord under Subsection (d), a judgment for court costs may be rendered against the landlord.

84

(g) A party may appeal from the court's judgment at the hearing on the sworn complaint for restoration of utility service in the same manner as a party may appeal a judgment in a forcible detainer suit.

(h) If a writ of possession is issued, it supersedes a writ of restoration of utility service.

(i) If the landlord or the person on whom a writ of restoration of utility service is served fails to immediately comply with the writ or later disobeys the writ, the failure is grounds for contempt of court against the landlord or the person on whom the writ was served under § 21.002, Government Code. If the writ is disobeyed, the tenant or the tenant's attorney may file in the court in which the action is pending an affidavit stating the name of the person who has disobeyed the writ and describing the acts or omissions constituting the disobedience. On receipt of an affidavit, the justice shall issue a show cause order, directing the person to appear on a designated date and show cause why the person should not be adjudged in contempt of court. If the justice finds, after considering the evidence at the hearing, that the person has directly or indirectly disobeyed the writ, the justice may commit the person to jail without bail until the person purges the contempt action or omission in a manner and form as the justice may direct. If the person disobeyed the writ before receiving the show cause order but has complied with the writ after receiving the order, the justice may find the person in contempt and assess punishment under § 21.002(c), Government Code.

(j) If a tenant in bad faith files a sworn complaint for restoration of utility service resulting in a writ being served on the landlord or landlord's agent, the landlord may in a separate cause of action recover from the tenant an amount equal to actual damages, one month's rent or $500, whichever is greater, reasonable attorney's fees, and costs of court, less any sums for which the landlord is liable to the tenant.

(k) The fee for filing a sworn complaint for restoration of utility service is the same as that for filing a civil action in justice court. The fee for service of a writ of restoration of utility service is the same as that for service of a writ of possession. The fee for service of a show cause order is the same as that for service of a civil citation. The justice may defer payment of the tenant's filing fees and service costs for the sworn complaint for restoration of utility service and writ of restoration of utility service. Court costs may be waived only if the tenant executes a pauper's affidavit.

§ 92.010 Occupancy limits

(a) Except as provided by Subsection (b), the maximum number of adults that a landlord may allow to occupy a dwelling is three times the number of bedrooms in the dwelling.

(b) A landlord may allow an occupancy rate of more than three adult tenants per bedroom:

(1) to the extent that the landlord is required by a state or federal fair housing law to allow a higher occupancy rate;   or

(2) if an adult whose occupancy causes a violation of Subsection (a) is seeking temporary sanctuary from family violence, as defined by § 71.004, Family Code, for a period that does not exceed one month.

(c) An individual who owns or leases a dwelling within 3,000 feet of a dwelling as to which a landlord has violated this section, or a governmental entity or civic association acting on behalf of the individual, may file suit against a landlord to enjoin the violation.   A party who prevails in a suit under this subsection may recover court costs and reasonable attorney's fees from the other party.   In addition to court costs and reasonable attorney's fees, a plaintiff who prevails under this subsection may recover from the landlord $500 for each violation of this section.

(d) In this section:

(1) "Adult" means an individual 18 years of age or older.

(2) "Bedroom" means an area of a dwelling intended as sleeping quarters.   The term does not include a kitchen, dining room, bathroom, living room, utility room, or closet or storage area of a dwelling.

§ 92.011 Cash rental payments

(a) A landlord shall accept a tenant's timely cash rental payment unless a written lease between the landlord and tenant requires the tenant to make rental payments by check, money order, or other traceable or negotiable instrument.

(b) A landlord who receives a cash rental payment shall:

(1) provide the tenant with a written receipt;   and

(2) enter the payment date and amount in a record book maintained by the landlord.

(c) A tenant or a governmental entity or civic association acting on the tenant's behalf may file suit against a landlord to enjoin a violation of this section.   A party who prevails in a suit brought under this subsection may recover court costs and reasonable attorney's fees from the other party.   In addition to court costs and reasonable attorney's fees, a tenant who prevails under this subsection may recover from the landlord the greater of one month's rent or $500 for each violation of this section.

§ 92.012 Notice to tenant at primary residence

(a) If, at the time of signing a lease or lease renewal, a tenant gives written notice to the tenant's landlord that the tenant does not occupy the leased premises as a primary residence and requests in writing that the landlord send notices to the tenant at the tenant's primary residence and provides to the landlord the address of the tenant's primary residence, the landlord shall mail to the tenant's primary residence:

(1) all notices of lease violations;

(2) all notices of lease termination;

(3) all notices of rental increases at the end of the lease term;   and

(4) all notices to vacate.

(b) The tenant shall notify the landlord in writing of any change in the tenant's primary residence address.   Oral notices of change are insufficient.

(c) A notice to a tenant's primary residence under Subsection (a) may be sent by regular United States mail and shall be considered as having been given on the date of postmark of the notice.

(d) If there is more than one tenant on a lease, the landlord is not required under this section to send notices to the primary residence of more than one tenant.

(e) This section does not apply if notice is actually hand delivered to and received by a person occupying the leased premises.

§ 92.013 Notice of rule or policy change affecting tenant's personal property

(a) A landlord shall give prior written notice to a tenant regarding a landlord rule or policy change that is not included in the lease agreement and that will affect any personal property owned by the tenant that is located outside the tenant's dwelling. A landlord shall provide to the tenant in a multiunit complex, as that term is defined by § 92.151, a copy of any applicable vehicle towing or parking rules or policies of the landlord and any changes to those rules or policies as provided by § 92.0131.

(b) The notice must be given in person or by mail to the affected tenant. Notice in person may be by personal delivery to the tenant or any person residing at the tenant's dwelling who is 16 years of age or older or by personal delivery to the tenant's dwelling and affixing the notice to the inside of the main entry door. Notice by mail may be by regular mail, by registered mail, or by certified mail, return receipt requested. If the dwelling has no mailbox and has a keyless bolting device, alarm system, or dangerous animal that prevents the landlord from entering the premises to leave the notice on the inside of the main entry door, the landlord may securely affix the notice on the outside of the main entry door.

(c) A landlord who fails to give notice as required by this section is liable to the tenant for any expense incurred by the tenant as a result of the landlord's failure to give the notice.

§ 92.0131 Notice regarding vehicle towing or parking rules or policies

(a) This section applies only to a tenant in a multiunit complex, as that term is defined by § 92.151.

(b) If at the time a lease agreement is executed a landlord has vehicle towing or parking rules or policies that apply to the tenant, the landlord shall provide to the tenant a copy of the rules or policies before the lease agreement is executed. The copy of the rules or policies must be:

(1) signed by the tenant;

(2) included in a lease agreement signed by the tenant; or

(3) included in an attachment to the lease agreement that is signed by the tenant, but only if the attachment is expressly referred to in the lease agreement.

(c) If the rules or policies are contained in the lease agreement or an attachment to the lease agreement, the title to the paragraph containing the rules or policies must read "Parking" or "Parking Rules" and be capitalized, underlined, or printed in bold print.

(c-1) As a precondition for allowing a tenant to park in a specific parking space or a common parking area that the landlord has made available for tenant use, the landlord may require a tenant to provide only the make, model, color, year, license number, and state of registration of the vehicle to be parked.

(c-2) Notwithstanding Subsection (c-1), a municipal housing authority located in a municipality that has a population of more than 500,000 and is not more than 50 miles from an international border, or a public facility corporation, affiliate, or subsidiary of the authority, may require that vehicles parked in a community of the authority, corporation, affiliate, or subsidiary be registered with the housing authority.

(d) If a landlord changes the vehicle towing or parking rules or policies during the term of the lease agreement, the landlord shall provide written notice of the change to the tenant before the tenant is required to comply with the rule or policy change. The landlord has the burden of proving that the tenant received a copy of the rule or policy change. The landlord may satisfy that burden of proof by providing evidence that the landlord:

(1) delivered the notice by certified mail, return receipt requested, addressed to the tenant at the tenant's dwelling; or

(2) made a notation in the landlord's files of the time, place, and method of providing the notice and the name of the person who delivered the notice by:

(A) hand delivery to the tenant or any occupant of the tenant's dwelling over the age of 16 years at the tenant's dwelling;

(B) facsimile to a facsimile number the tenant provided to the landlord for the purpose of receiving notices; or

(C) taping the notice to the inside of the main entry door of the tenant's dwelling.

(e) If a rule or policy change is made during the term of the lease agreement, the change:

(1) must:

(A) apply to all of the landlord's tenants in the same multiunit complex and be based on necessity, safety or security of tenants, reasonable requirements for construction on the premises, or respect for other tenants' parking rights; or

(B) be adopted based on the tenant's written consent; and

(2) may not be effective before the 14th day after the date notice of the change is delivered to the tenant, unless the change is the result of a construction or utility emergency.

(f) A landlord who violates Subsection (b), (c), (d), or (e) is liable for a civil penalty in the amount of $100 plus any towing or storage costs that the tenant incurs as a result of the towing of the tenant's vehicle. The nonprevailing party in a suit under this section is liable to the prevailing party for reasonable attorney's fees and court costs.

(g) A landlord is liable for any damage to a tenant's vehicle resulting from the negligence of a towing service that contracts with the landlord or the landlord's agent to remove vehicles that are parked in violation of the landlord's rules and policies if the towing company that caused the damage does not carry insurance that covers the damage.

§ 92.0132 Term of parking permit
    A landlord who issues a parking permit to a tenant:
(1) must issue the permit for a term that is coterminous with the tenant's lease term; and
(2) may not terminate or suspend the permit until the date the tenant's right of possession ends.

§ 92.0135 Notice for dwelling located in floodplain
    (a) In this section:
        (1) "100-year floodplain" means any area of land designated as a flood hazard area with a one percent or greater chance of flooding each year by the Federal Emergency Management Agency under the National Flood Insurance Act of 1968 (42 U.S.C. § 4001 *et seq.*).
        (2) "Flooding" means a general or temporary condition of partial or complete inundation of a dwelling caused by:
            (A) the overflow of inland or tidal waters;
            (B) the unusual and rapid accumulation of runoff or surface waters from any established water source such as a river, stream, or drainage ditch; or
            (C) excessive rainfall.
    (b) A landlord shall provide to a tenant a written notice substantially equivalent to the following:
    "(Landlord) ( ) is or ( ) is not aware that the dwelling you are renting is located in a 100-year floodplain.   If neither box is checked, you should assume the dwelling is in a 100-year floodplain.   Even if the dwelling is not in a 100-year floodplain, the dwelling may still be susceptible to flooding. The Federal Emergency Management Agency (FEMA) maintains a flood map on its Internet website that is searchable by address, at no cost, to determine if a dwelling is located in a flood hazard area. Most tenant insurance policies do not cover damages or loss incurred in a flood.   You should seek insurance coverage that would cover losses caused by a flood."
    (c) Notwithstanding Subsection (b), a landlord is not required to disclose on the notice that the landlord is aware that a dwelling is located in a 100-year floodplain if the elevation of the dwelling is raised above the 100-year floodplain flood levels in accordance with federal regulations.
    (d) If a landlord knows that flooding has damaged any portion of a dwelling at least once during the five-year period immediately preceding the

effective date of the lease, the landlord shall provide a written notice to a tenant that is substantially equivalent to the following:

"(Landlord) ( ) is or ( ) is not aware that the dwelling you are renting has flooded at least once within the last five years."

(e) The notices required by Subsections (b) and (d) must be included in a separate written document given to the tenant at or before execution of the lease.

(f) If a landlord violates this section and a tenant suffers a substantial loss or damage to the tenant's personal property as a result of flooding, the tenant may terminate the lease by giving a written notice of termination to the landlord not later than the 30th day after the date the loss or damage occurred. For purposes of this subsection, a tenant suffers a substantial loss or damage to personal property if the total cost of repairs to or replacement of the personal property is 50 percent or more of the personal property's market value on the date the flooding occurred.   Termination of a lease under this subsection is effective when the tenant surrenders possession of the dwelling.

(g) Not later than the 30th day after the effective date of the termination of a lease under Subsection (f), the landlord shall refund to the tenant all rent or other amounts paid in advance under the lease for any period after the effective date of the termination of the lease.

(h) This section does not affect a tenant's liability for delinquent, unpaid rent or other sums owed to the landlord before the date the lease was terminated by the tenant under this section.

§ 92.014 Personal property and security deposit of deceased tenant

(a) Upon written request of a landlord, the landlord's tenant shall:

(1) provide the landlord with the name, address, and telephone number of a person to contact in the event of the tenant's death;   and

(2) sign a statement authorizing the landlord in the event of the tenant's death to:

(A) grant to the person designated under Subdivision (1) access to the premises at a reasonable time and in the presence of the landlord or the landlord's agent;

(B) allow the person designated under Subdivision (1) to remove any of the tenant's property found at the leased premises;   and

(C) refund the tenant's security deposit, less lawful deductions, to the person designated under Subdivision (1).

(b) A tenant may, without request from the landlord, provide the landlord with the information in Subsection (a).

(c) Except as provided in Subsection (d), in the event of the death of a tenant who is the sole occupant of a rental dwelling:

(1) the landlord may remove and store all property found in the tenant's leased premises;

(2) the landlord shall turn over possession of the property to the person who was designated by the tenant under Subsection (a) or (b) or to any other person lawfully entitled to the property if the request is made prior to the property being discarded under Subdivision (5);

(3) the landlord shall refund the tenant's security deposit, less lawful deductions, including the cost of removing and storing the property, to the person designated under Subsection (a) or (b) or to any other person lawfully entitled to the refund;

(4) the landlord may require any person who removes the property from the tenant's leased premises to sign an inventory of the property being removed;   and

(5) the landlord may discard the property removed by the landlord from the tenant's leased premises if:

(A) the landlord has mailed a written request by certified mail, return receipt requested, to the person designated under Subsection (a) or (b), requesting that the property be removed;

(B) the person failed to remove the property by the 30th day after the postmark date of the notice; and

(C) the landlord, prior to the date of discarding the property, has not been contacted by anyone claiming the property.

(d) In a written lease or other agreement, a landlord and a tenant may agree to a procedure different than the procedure in this section for removing, storing, or disposing of property in the leased premises of a deceased tenant.

(e) If a tenant, after being furnished with a copy of this subchapter, knowingly violates Subsection (a), the landlord shall have no responsibility after the tenant's death for removal, storage, disappearance, damage, or disposition of property in the tenant's leased premises.

(f) If a landlord, after being furnished with a copy of this subchapter, knowingly violates Subsection (c), the landlord shall be liable to the estate of the deceased tenant for actual damages.

§ 92.015 Tenant's right to summon police or emergency assistance

(a) A landlord may not:

(1) prohibit or limit a residential tenant's right to summon police or other emergency assistance in response to family violence; or

(2) impose monetary or other penalties on a tenant who summons police or emergency assistance in response to family violence.

(b) A provision in a lease is void if the provision purports to:

(1) waive a tenant's right to summon police or other emergency assistance in response to family violence; or

(2) exempt any party from a liability or a duty under this section.

(c) In addition to other remedies provided by law, if a landlord violates this section, a tenant is entitled to recover from or against the landlord:

(1) a civil penalty in an amount equal to one month's rent;

(2) actual damages suffered by the tenant as a result of the landlord's violation of this section;

(3) court costs;

(4) injunctive relief; and

(5) reasonable attorney's fees incurred by the tenant in seeking enforcement of this section.

(d) For purposes of this section, if a tenant's rent is subsidized in whole or in part by a governmental entity, "one month's rent" means one month's fair market rent.

(e) For purposes of this section, "family violence" has the meaning assigned by § 71.004, Family Code.

§ 92.016 Right to vacate and avoid liability following family violence

(a) For purposes of this section:

(1) "Family violence" has the meaning assigned by § 71.004, Family Code.

(2) "Occupant" means a person who has the landlord's consent to occupy a dwelling but has no obligation to pay the rent for the dwelling.

(b) A tenant may terminate the tenant's rights and obligations under a lease and may vacate the dwelling and avoid liability for future rent and any other sums due under the lease for terminating the lease and vacating the dwelling before the end of the lease term if the tenant complies with Subsection (c) and provides the landlord or the landlord's agent a copy of one or more of the following orders protecting the tenant or an occupant from family violence:

(1) a temporary injunction issued under Subchapter F, Chapter 6, Family Code;

(2) a temporary ex parte order issued under Chapter 83, Family Code; or

(3) a protective order issued under Chapter 85, Family Code.

(c) A tenant may exercise the rights to terminate the lease under Subsection (b), vacate the dwelling before the end of the lease term, and avoid liability beginning on the date after all of the following events have occurred:

(1) a judge signs an order described by Subsection (b);

(2) the tenant provides a copy of the relevant documentation described by Subsection (b) to the landlord;

(3) the tenant provides written notice of termination of the lease to the landlord on or before the 30th day before the date the lease terminates;

(4) the 30th day after the date the tenant provided notice under Subdivision (3) expires; and

(5) the tenant vacates the dwelling.

(c-1) If the family violence is committed by a cotenant or occupant of the dwelling, a tenant may exercise the right to terminate the lease under the procedures provided by Subsection (b)(1) or (3) and Subsection (c), except that the tenant is not required to provide the notice described by Subsection (c)(3).

(d) Except as provided by Subsection (f), this section does not affect a tenant's liability for delinquent, unpaid rent or other sums owed to the landlord before the lease was terminated by the tenant under this section.

(e) A landlord who violates this section is liable to the tenant for actual damages, a civil penalty equal in amount to the amount of one month's rent plus $500, and attorney's fees.

(f) A tenant who terminates a lease under Subsection (b) is released from all liability for any delinquent, unpaid rent owed to the landlord by the tenant on the effective date of the lease termination if the lease does not contain language substantially equivalent to the following:

"Tenants may have special statutory rights to terminate the lease early in certain situations involving family violence or a military deployment or transfer."

(g) A tenant's right to terminate a lease before the end of the lease term, vacate the dwelling, and avoid liability under this section may not be waived by a tenant.

§ 92.0161 Right to vacate and avoid liability following certain sex offenses or stalking

(a) In this section, "occupant" has the meaning assigned by § 92.016.

(b) A tenant may terminate the tenant's rights and obligations under a lease and may vacate the dwelling and avoid liability for future rent and any other sums due under the lease for terminating the lease and vacating the dwelling before the end of the lease term after the tenant complies with Subsection (c) or (c-1).

(c) If the tenant is a victim or a parent or guardian of a victim of sexual assault under § 22.011, Penal Code, aggravated sexual assault under § 22.021, Penal Code, indecency with a child under § 21.11, Penal Code, sexual performance by a child under § 43.25, Penal Code, continuous sexual abuse of a child under § 21.02, Penal Code, or an attempt to commit any of the foregoing offenses under § 15.01, Penal Code, that takes place during the preceding six-month period on the premises or at any dwelling on the premises, the tenant shall provide to the landlord or the landlord's agent a copy of:

(1) documentation of the assault or abuse, or attempted assault or abuse, of the victim from a licensed health care services provider who examined the victim;

(2) documentation of the assault or abuse, or attempted assault or abuse, of the victim from a licensed mental health services provider who examined or evaluated the victim;

(3) documentation of the assault or abuse, or attempted assault or abuse, of the victim from an individual authorized under Chapter 420, Government Code, who provided services to the victim; or

(4) documentation of a protective order issued under Subchapter A, Chapter 7B, Code of Criminal Procedure, except for a temporary ex parte order.

(c-1) If the tenant is a victim or a parent or guardian of a victim of stalking under § 42.072, Penal Code, that takes place during the preceding six-month period on the premises or at any dwelling on the premises, the tenant shall provide to the landlord or the landlord's agent a copy of:

(1) documentation of a protective order issued under Subchapter A or B, Chapter 7B, Code of Criminal Procedure, except for a temporary ex parte order; or

(2) documentation of the stalking from a provider of services described by Subsection (c)(1), (2), or (3) and:

(A) a law enforcement incident report or, if a law enforcement incident report is unavailable, another record maintained in the ordinary course of business by a law enforcement agency; and

(B) if the report or record described by Paragraph (A) identifies the victim by means of a pseudonym, as defined by Article 58.001, Code of Criminal Procedure, a copy of a pseudonym form completed and returned under Article 58.152(a) of that code.

(d) A tenant may exercise the rights to terminate the lease under Subsection (b), vacate the dwelling before the end of the lease term, and avoid liability beginning on the date after all of the following events have occurred:

(1) the tenant provides a copy of the relevant documentation described by Subsection (c) or (c-1) to the landlord;

(2) the tenant provides written notice of termination of the lease to the landlord on or before the 30th day before the date the lease terminates;

(3) the 30th day after the date the tenant provided notice under Subdivision (2) expires; and

(4) the tenant vacates the dwelling.

(e) Except as provided by Subsection (g), this section does not affect a tenant's liability for delinquent, unpaid rent or other sums owed to the landlord before the lease was terminated by the tenant under this section.

(f) A landlord who violates this section is liable to the tenant for actual damages, a civil penalty equal to the amount of one month's rent plus $500, and attorney's fees.

(g) A tenant who terminates a lease under Subsection (b) is released from all liability for any delinquent, unpaid rent owed to the landlord by the tenant on the effective date of the lease termination if the lease does not contain language substantially equivalent to the following:

"Tenants may have special statutory rights to terminate the lease early in certain situations involving certain sexual offenses or stalking."

(h) A tenant may not waive a tenant's right to terminate a lease before the end of the lease term, vacate the dwelling, and avoid liability under this chapter.

(i) For purposes of Subsections (c) and (c-1), a tenant who is a parent or guardian of a victim described by those subsections must reside with the victim to exercise the rights established by this section.

(j) A person who receives information under Subsection (c), (c-1), or (d) may not disclose the information to any other person except for a legitimate or customary business purpose or as otherwise required by law.

§ 92.017 Right to vacate and avoid liability following certain decisions related to military service

(a) For purposes of this section, "dependent," "military service," and "servicemember" have the meanings assigned by 50 App. U.S.C. § 511.

(b) A tenant who is a servicemember or a dependent of a servicemember may vacate the dwelling leased by the tenant and avoid liability for future rent and all other sums due under the lease for terminating the lease and vacating the dwelling before the end of the lease term if:

(1) the lease was executed by or on behalf of a person who, after executing the lease or during the term of the lease, enters military service; or

(2) a servicemember, while in military service, executes the lease and after executing the lease receives military orders:

(A) for a permanent change of station; or

(B) to deploy with a military unit for a period of 90 days or more.

(c) A tenant who terminates a lease under Subsection (b) shall deliver to the landlord or landlord's agent:

(1) a written notice of termination of the lease; and

(2) a copy of an appropriate government document providing evidence of the tenant's entrance into military service if Subsection (b)(1) applies or a copy of the servicemember's military orders if Subsection (b)(2) applies.

(d) Termination of a lease under this section is effective:

(1) in the case of a lease that provides for monthly payment of rent, on the 30th day after the first date on which the next rental payment is due after the date on which the notice under Subsection (c)(1) is delivered; or

(2) in the case of a lease other than a lease described by Subdivision (1), on the last day of the month following the month in which the notice under Subsection (c)(1) is delivered.

(e) A landlord, not later than the 30th day after the effective date of the termination of a lease under this section, shall refund to the residential tenant terminating the lease under Subsection (b) all rent or other amounts paid in advance under the lease for any period after the effective date of the termination of the lease.

(f) Except as provided by Subsection (g), this section does not affect a tenant's liability for delinquent, unpaid rent or other sums owed to the landlord before the lease was terminated by the tenant under this section.

(g) A tenant who terminates a lease under Subsection (b) is released from all liability for any delinquent, unpaid rent owed to the landlord by the tenant on the effective date of the lease termination if the lease does not contain language substantially equivalent to the following:

"Tenants may have special statutory rights to terminate the lease early in certain situations involving family violence or a military deployment or transfer."

(h) A landlord who violates this section is liable to the tenant for actual damages, a civil penalty in an amount equal to the amount of one month's rent plus $500, and attorney's fees.

(i) Except as provided by Subsection (j), a tenant's right to terminate a lease before the end of the lease term, vacate the dwelling, and avoid liability under this section may not be waived by a tenant.

(j) A tenant and a landlord may agree that the tenant waives a tenant's rights under this section if the tenant or any dependent living with the tenant moves into base housing or other housing within 30 miles of the dwelling. A waiver under this section must be signed and in writing in a document separate from the lease and must comply with federal law. A waiver under this section does not apply if:

(1) the tenant or the tenant's dependent moves into housing owned or occupied by family or relatives of the tenant or the tenant's dependent; or

(2) the tenant and the tenant's dependent move, wholly or partly, because of a significant financial loss of income caused by the tenant's military service.

(k) For purposes of Subsection (j), "significant financial loss of income" means a reduction of 10 percent or more of the tenant's household income caused by the tenant's military service. A landlord is entitled to verify the significant financial loss of income in order to determine whether a tenant is entitled to terminate a lease if the tenant has signed a waiver under this section and moves within 30 miles of the dwelling into housing that is not owned or occupied by family or relatives of the tenant or the tenant's dependent. For purposes of this subsection, a pay stub or other statement of earnings issued by the tenant's employer is sufficient verification.

§ 92.018 Liability of tenant for governmental fines

(a) In this section, "governmental entity" means the state, an agency of the state, or a political subdivision of the state.

(b) A landlord or a landlord's manager or agent may not charge or seek reimbursement from the landlord's tenant for the amount of a fine imposed on the landlord by a governmental entity unless the tenant or another occupant of the tenant's dwelling actually caused the damage or other condition on which the fine is based.

§ 92.019 Late payment of rent; fees

(a) A landlord may not charge a tenant a late fee for failing to pay rent unless:

(1) notice of the fee is included in a written lease;

(2) the fee is a reasonable estimate of uncertain damages to the landlord that are incapable of precise calculation and result from late payment of rent; and

(3) the rent has remained unpaid one full day after the date the rent was originally due.

(b) A late fee under this section may include an initial fee and a daily fee for each day the rent continues to remain unpaid.

(c) A landlord who violates this section is liable to the tenant for an amount equal to the sum of $100, three times the amount of the late fee charged in violation of this section, and the tenant's reasonable attorney's fees.

(d) A provision of a lease that purports to waive a right or exempt a party from a liability or duty under this section is void.

(e) This section relates only to a fee, charge, or other sum of money required to be paid under the lease if rent is not paid as provided by Subsection (a)(3), and does not affect the landlord's right to terminate the lease or take other action permitted by the lease or other law. Payment of the fee, charge, or other sum of money by a tenant does not waive the right or remedies provided by this section.

§ 92.020 Emergency phone number

(a) A landlord that has an on-site management or superintendent's office for a residential rental property must provide to a tenant a telephone number that will be answered 24 hours a day for the purpose of reporting emergencies related to a condition of the leased premises that materially affects the physical health or safety of an ordinary tenant.

(b) The landlord must post the phone number required by Subsection (a) prominently outside the management or superintendent's office.

(c) This section does not apply to or affect a local ordinance governing a landlord's obligation to provide a 24-hour emergency contact number to a tenant that is adopted before January 1, 2008, if the ordinance conforms with or is amended to conform with this section.

(d) A landlord to whom Subsection (a) does not apply must provide to a tenant a telephone number for the purpose of reporting emergencies described by that subsection.

§ 92.021 Liability of certain guarantors under lease

(a)   A person other than a tenant who guarantees a lease is liable only for the original lease term except that a person may specify that the person agrees to guarantee a renewal of the lease as provided by Subsection (b).

(b) A person may specify in writing in an original lease that the person will guarantee a renewal of the lease only if the original lease states:

(1) the last date, as specified by the guarantor, on which the renewal of the lease will renew the obligation of the guarantor;

(2) that the guarantor is liable under a renewal of the lease that occurs on or before that date; and

(3) that the guarantor is liable under a renewal of the lease only if the renewal:

(A) involves the same parties as the original lease; and

(B) does not increase the guarantor's potential financial obligation for rent that existed under the original lease.

(c) Subsection (b) does not prohibit a guarantor from voluntarily entering into an agreement at the time of the renewal of a lease, in a separate written document, to guarantee an increased amount of rent.

(d) This section does not release a guarantor from the obligations of the guarantor under the terms of the original lease or a valid renewal for costs and damages owed to the lessor that arise after the date specified by the guarantor in the original lease in accordance with Subsection (b), if the costs or damages relate to actions of the tenant before that date or arise as a result of the tenant refusing to vacate the leased premises.

§ 92.023 Tenant's remedies regarding revocation of certificate of occupancy

If a municipality or a county revokes a certificate of occupancy for a leased premises because of the landlord's failure to maintain the premises, the landlord is liable to a tenant who is not in default under the lease for:

(1) the full amount of the tenant's security deposit;

(2) the pro rata portion of any rental payment the tenant has paid in advance;

(3) the tenant's actual damages, including any moving costs, utility connection fees, storage fees, and lost wages; and

(4) court costs and attorney's fees arising from any related cause of action by the tenant against the landlord.

§ 92.024 Landlord's duty to provide copy of lease
(a) Not later than the third business day after the date the lease is signed by each party to the lease, a landlord shall provide at least one complete copy of the lease to at least one tenant who is a party to the lease.
(b) If more than one tenant is a party to the lease, not later than the third business day after the date a landlord receives a written request for a copy of a lease from a tenant who has not received a copy of the lease under Subsection (a), the landlord shall provide one complete copy of the lease to the requesting tenant.
(c) A landlord's failure to provide a complete copy of the lease as described by Subsection (a) or (b) does not invalidate the lease or, subject to Subsection (d), prevent the landlord from prosecuting or defending a legal action or proceeding to enforce the lease.
(d) A landlord may not continue to prosecute and a court shall abate an action to enforce the lease, other than an action for nonpayment of rent, only until the landlord provides to a tenant a complete copy of the lease if the tenant submits to the court evidence in a plea in abatement or otherwise that the landlord failed to comply with Subsection (a) or (b).
(e) A landlord may comply with this section by providing to a tenant a complete copy of the lease:
(1) in a paper format;
(2) in an electronic format if requested by the tenant; or
(3) by e-mail if the parties have communicated by e-mail regarding the lease.

SUBCHAPTER B: REPAIR OR CLOSING OF LEASEHOLD

§ 92.051 Application
   This subchapter applies to a lease executed, entered into, renewed, or extended on or after September 1, 1979.

§ 92.052 Landlord's duty to repair or remedy
   (a) A landlord shall make a diligent effort to repair or remedy a condition if:
      (1) the tenant specifies the condition in a notice to the person to whom or to the place where rent is normally paid;
      (2) the tenant is not delinquent in the payment of rent at the time notice is given; and
      (3) the condition:
         (A) materially affects the physical health or safety of an ordinary tenant; or
         (B) arises from the landlord's failure to provide and maintain in good operating condition a device to supply hot water of a minimum temperature of 120 degrees Fahrenheit.
   (b) Unless the condition was caused by normal wear and tear, the landlord does not have a duty during the lease term or a renewal or extension to repair or remedy a condition caused by:
      (1) the tenant;
      (2) a lawful occupant in the tenant's dwelling;
      (3) a member of the tenant's family; or
      (4) a guest or invitee of the tenant.
   (c) This subchapter does not require the landlord:
      (1) to furnish utilities from a utility company if as a practical matter the utility lines of the company are not reasonably available;   or
      (2) to furnish security guards.
   (d) The tenant's notice under Subsection (a) must be in writing only if the tenant's lease is in writing and requires written notice.

§ 92.053 Burden of proof
   (a)   Except as provided by this section, the tenant has the burden of proof in a judicial action to enforce a right resulting from the landlord's failure to repair or remedy a condition under § 92.052.

(b) If the landlord does not provide a written explanation for delay in performing a duty to repair or remedy on or before the fifth day after receiving from the tenant a written demand for an explanation, the landlord has the burden of proving that he made a diligent effort to repair and that a reasonable time for repair did not elapse.

§ 92.054 Casualty loss
(a)   If a condition results from an insured casualty loss, such as fire, smoke, hail, explosion, or a similar cause, the period for repair does not begin until the landlord receives the insurance proceeds.
(b) If after a casualty loss the rental premises are as a practical matter totally unusable for residential purposes and if the casualty loss is not caused by the negligence or fault of the tenant, a member of the tenant's family, or a guest or invitee of the tenant, either the landlord or the tenant may terminate the lease by giving written notice to the other any time before repairs are completed.   If the lease is terminated, the tenant is entitled only to a pro rata refund of rent from the date the tenant moves out and to a refund of any security deposit otherwise required by law.
(c) If after a casualty loss the rental premises are partially unusable for residential purposes and if the casualty loss is not caused by the negligence or fault of the tenant, a member of the tenant's family, or a guest or invitee of the tenant, the tenant is entitled to reduction in the rent in an amount proportionate to the extent the premises are unusable because of the casualty, but only on judgment of a county or district court.   A landlord and tenant may agree otherwise in a written lease.

§ 92.055 Closing the rental premises
(a) A landlord may close a rental unit at any time by giving written notice by certified mail, return receipt requested, to the tenant and to the local health officer and local building inspector, if any, stating that:
(1) the landlord is terminating the tenancy as soon as legally possible; and
(2) after the tenant moves out the landlord will either immediately demolish the rental unit or no longer use the unit for residential purposes.
(b) After a tenant receives the notice and moves out:
(1) the local health officer or building inspector may not allow occupancy of or utility service by separate meter to the rental unit until the

officer certifies that he knows of no condition that materially affects the physical health or safety of an ordinary tenant; and

(2) the landlord may not allow reoccupancy or reconnection of utilities by separate meter within six months after the date the tenant moves out.

(c) If the landlord gives the tenant the notice closing the rental unit:

(1) before the tenant gives a repair notice to the landlord, the remedies of this subchapter do not apply;

(2) after the tenant gives a repair notice to the landlord but before the landlord has had a reasonable time to make repairs, the tenant is entitled only to the remedies under Subsection (d) of this section and Subdivisions (3), (4), and (5) of Subsection (a) of § 92.0563; or

(3) after the tenant gives a repair notice to the landlord and after the landlord has had a reasonable time to make repairs, the tenant is entitled only to the remedies under Subsection (d) of this section and Subdivisions (3), (4), and (5) of Subsection (a) of § 92.0563.

(d) If the landlord closes the rental unit after the tenant gives the landlord a notice to repair and the tenant moves out on or before the end of the rental term, the landlord must pay the tenant's actual and reasonable moving expenses, refund a pro rata portion of the tenant's rent from the date the tenant moves out, and, if otherwise required by law, return the tenant's security deposit.

(e) A landlord who violates Subsection (b) or (d) is liable to the tenant for an amount equal to the total of one month's rent plus $100 and attorney's fees.

(f) The closing of a rental unit does not prohibit the occupancy of other apartments, nor does this subchapter prohibit occupancy of or utility service by master or individual meter to other rental units in an apartment complex that have not been closed under this section.   If another provision of this subchapter conflicts with this section, this section controls.

§ 92.056 Landlord liability and tenant remedies; notice and time for repair

(a) A landlord's liability under this section is subject to § 92.052(b) regarding conditions that are caused by a tenant and § 92.054 regarding conditions that are insured casualties.

(b) A landlord is liable to a tenant as provided by this subchapter if:

(1) the tenant has given the landlord notice to repair or remedy a condition by giving that notice to the person to whom or to the place where the tenant's rent is normally paid;

(2) the condition materially affects the physical health or safety of an ordinary tenant;

(3) the tenant has given the landlord a subsequent written notice to repair or remedy the condition after a reasonable time to repair or remedy the condition following the notice given under Subdivision (1) or the tenant has given the notice under Subdivision (1) by sending that notice by certified mail, return receipt requested, or by registered mail;

(4) the landlord has had a reasonable time to repair or remedy the condition after the landlord received the tenant's notice under Subdivision (1) and, if applicable, the tenant's subsequent notice under Subdivision (3);

(5) the landlord has not made a diligent effort to repair or remedy the condition after the landlord received the tenant's notice under Subdivision (1) and, if applicable, the tenant's notice under Subdivision (3); and

(6) the tenant was not delinquent in the payment of rent at the time any notice required by this subsection was given.

(c) For purposes of Subsection (b)(4) or (5), a landlord is considered to have received the tenant's notice when the landlord or the landlord's agent or employee has actually received the notice or when the United States Postal Service has attempted to deliver the notice to the landlord.

(d) For purposes of Subsection (b)(3) or (4), in determining whether a period of time is a reasonable time to repair or remedy a condition, there is a rebuttable presumption that seven days is a reasonable time.   To rebut that presumption, the date on which the landlord received the tenant's notice, the severity and nature of the condition, and the reasonable availability of materials and labor and of utilities from a utility company must be considered.

(e) Except as provided in Subsection (f), a tenant to whom a landlord is liable under Subsection (b) of this section may:

(1) terminate the lease;

(2) have the condition repaired or remedied according to § 92.0561;

(3) deduct from the tenant's rent, without necessity of judicial action, the cost of the repair or remedy according to § 92.0561;   and

(4) obtain judicial remedies according to § 92.0563.

(f) A tenant who elects to terminate the lease under Subsection (e) is:

(1) entitled to a pro rata refund of rent from the date of termination or the date the tenant moves out, whichever is later;

(2) entitled to deduct the tenant's security deposit from the tenant's rent without necessity of lawsuit or obtain a refund of the tenant's security deposit according to law; and

(3) not entitled to the other repair and deduct remedies under § 92.0561 or the judicial remedies under Subdivisions (1) and (2) of Subsection (a) of § 92.0563.

(g) A lease must contain language in underlined or bold print that informs the tenant of the remedies available under this section and § 92.0561.

§ 92.0561 Tenant's repair and deduct remedies

(a) If the landlord is liable to the tenant under § 92.056(b), the tenant may have the condition repaired or remedied and may deduct the cost from a subsequent rent payment as provided in this section.

(b) The tenant's deduction for the cost of the repair or remedy may not exceed the amount of one month's rent under the lease or $500, whichever is greater. However, if the tenant's rent is subsidized in whole or in part by a governmental agency, the deduction limitation of one month's rent shall mean the fair market rent for the dwelling and not the rent that the tenant pays. The fair market rent shall be determined by the governmental agency subsidizing the rent, or in the absence of such a determination, it shall be a reasonable amount of rent under the circumstances.

(c) Repairs and deductions under this section may be made as often as necessary so long as the total repairs and deductions in any one month do not exceed one month's rent or $500, whichever is greater.

(d) Repairs under this section may be made only if all of the following requirements are met:

(1) The landlord has a duty to repair or remedy the condition under § 92.052, and the duty has not been waived in a written lease by the tenant under Subsection (e) or (f) of § 92.006.

(2) The tenant has given notice to the landlord as required by § 92.056(b)(1), and, if required, a subsequent notice under § 92.056(b)(3), and at least one of those notices states that the tenant intends to repair or remedy the condition. The notice shall also contain a reasonable description of the intended repair or remedy.

(3) Any one of the following events has occurred:

(A) The landlord has failed to remedy the backup or overflow of raw sewage inside the tenant's dwelling or the flooding from broken pipes or natural drainage inside the dwelling.

(B) The landlord has expressly or impliedly agreed in the lease to furnish potable water to the tenant's dwelling and the water service to the dwelling has totally ceased.

(C) The landlord has expressly or impliedly agreed in the lease to furnish heating or cooling equipment; the equipment is producing inadequate heat or cooled air;   and the landlord has been notified in writing by the appropriate local housing, building, or health official or other official having jurisdiction that the lack of heat or cooling materially affects the health or safety of an ordinary tenant.

(D) The landlord has been notified in writing by the appropriate local housing, building, or health official or other official having jurisdiction that the condition materially affects the health or safety of an ordinary tenant.

(e) If the requirements of Subsection (d) of this section are met, a tenant may:

(1) have the condition repaired or remedied immediately following the tenant's notice of intent to repair if the condition involves sewage or flooding as referred to in Paragraph (A) of Subdivision (3) of Subsection (d) of this section;

(2) have the condition repaired or remedied if the condition involves a cessation of potable water as referred to in Paragraph (A) of Subdivision (3) of Subsection (d) of this section and if the landlord has failed to repair or remedy the condition within three days following the tenant's delivery of notice of intent to repair;

(3) have the condition repaired or remedied if the condition involves inadequate heat or cooled air as referred to in Paragraph (C) of Subdivision (3) of Subsection (d) of this section and if the landlord has failed to repair the condition within three days after delivery of the tenant's notice of intent to repair; or

(4) have the condition repaired or remedied if the condition is not covered by Paragraph (A), (B), or (C) of Subdivision (3) of Subsection (d) of this section and involves a condition affecting the physical health or safety of the ordinary tenant as referred to in Paragraph (D) of Subdivision (3) of Subsection (d) of this section and if the landlord has failed to repair or remedy the condition within seven days after delivery of the tenant's notice of intent to repair.

(f) Repairs made pursuant to the tenant's notice must be made by a company, contractor, or repairman listed in the yellow or business pages of the telephone directory or in the classified advertising section of a newspaper of the local city, county, or adjacent county at the time of the tenant's notice of intent to repair.   Unless the landlord and tenant agree otherwise under Subsection (g) of this section, repairs may not be made by the tenant, the tenant's immediate family, the tenant's employer or employees, or a company in which the tenant has an ownership interest. Repairs may not be made to the foundation or load-bearing structural elements of the building if it contains two or more dwelling units.

(g) A landlord and a tenant may mutually agree for the tenant to repair or remedy, at the landlord's expense, any condition of the dwelling regardless of whether it materially affects the health or safety of an ordinary tenant. However, the landlord's duty to repair or remedy conditions covered by this subchapter may not be waived except as provided by Subsection (e) or (f) of § 92.006.

(h) Repairs made pursuant to the tenant's notice must be made in compliance with applicable building codes, including a building permit when required.

(i) The tenant shall not have authority to contract for labor or materials in excess of what the tenant may deduct under this section. The landlord is not liable to repairmen, contractors, or material suppliers who furnish labor or materials to repair or remedy the condition. A repairman or supplier shall not have a lien for materials or services arising out of repairs contracted for by the tenant under this section.

(j) When deducting the cost of repairs from the rent payment, the tenant shall furnish the landlord, along with payment of the balance of the rent, a copy of the repair bill and the receipt for its payment. A repair bill and receipt may be the same document.

(k) If the landlord repairs or remedies the condition or delivers an affidavit for delay under § 92.0562 to the tenant after the tenant has contacted a repairman but before the repairman commences work, the landlord shall be liable for the cost incurred by the tenant for the repairman's trip charge, and the tenant may deduct the charge from the tenant's rent as if it were a repair cost.

§ 92.0562 Landlord affidavit for delay

(a) The tenant must delay contracting for repairs under § 92.0561 if, before the tenant contracts for the repairs, the landlord delivers to the tenant an affidavit, signed and sworn to under oath by the landlord or his authorized agent and complying with this section.

(b) The affidavit must summarize the reasons for the delay and the diligent efforts made by the landlord up to the date of the affidavit to get the repairs done. The affidavit must state facts showing that the landlord has made and is making diligent efforts to repair the condition, and it must contain dates, names, addresses, and telephone numbers of contractors, suppliers, and repairmen contacted by the owner.

(c) Affidavits under this section may delay repair by the tenant for:

(1) 15 days if the landlord's failure to repair is caused by a delay in obtaining necessary parts for which the landlord is not at fault;   or

(2) 30 days if the landlord's failure to repair is caused by a general shortage of labor or materials for repair following a natural disaster such as a hurricane, tornado, flood, extended freeze, or widespread windstorm.

(d) Affidavits for delay based on grounds other than those listed in Subsection (c) of this section are unlawful, and if used, they are of no effect. The landlord may file subsequent affidavits, provided that the total delay of the repair or remedy extends no longer than six months from the date the landlord delivers the first affidavit to the tenant.

(e) The affidavit must be delivered to the tenant by any of the following methods:

(1) personal delivery to the tenant;

(2) certified mail, return receipt requested, to the tenant; or

(3) leaving the notice inside the dwelling in a conspicuous place if notice in that manner is authorized in a written lease.

(f) Affidavits for delay by a landlord under this section must be submitted in good faith.   Following delivery of the affidavit, the landlord must continue diligent efforts to repair or remedy the condition.   There shall be a rebuttable presumption that the landlord acted in good faith and with continued diligence for the first affidavit for delay the landlord delivers to the tenant. The landlord shall have the burden of pleading and proving good faith and continued diligence for subsequent affidavits for delay.   A landlord who violates this section shall be liable to the tenant for all judicial remedies under § 92.0563 except that the civil penalty under Subdivision (3) of Subsection (a) of § 92.0563 shall be one month's rent plus $1,000.

(g) If the landlord is liable to the tenant under § 92.056 and if a new landlord, in good faith and without knowledge of the tenant's notice of intent to repair, has acquired title to the tenant's dwelling by foreclosure, deed in lieu of foreclosure, or general warranty deed in a bona fide purchase, then the following shall apply:

(1) The tenant's right to terminate the lease under this subchapter shall not be affected, and the tenant shall have no duty to give additional notice to the new landlord.

(2) The tenant's right to repair and deduct for conditions involving sewage backup or overflow, flooding inside the dwelling, or a cutoff of

potable water under Subsection (e) of § 92.0561 shall not be affected, and the tenant shall have no duty to give additional notice to the new landlord.

(3) For conditions other than those specified in Subdivision (2) of this subsection, if the new landlord acquires title as described in this subsection and has notified the tenant of the name and address of the new landlord or the new landlord's authorized agent and if the tenant has not already contracted for the repair or remedy at the time the tenant is so notified, the tenant must deliver to the new landlord a written notice of intent to repair or remedy the condition, and the new landlord shall have a reasonable time to complete the repair before the tenant may repair or remedy the condition. No further notice from the tenant is necessary in order for the tenant to repair or remedy the condition after a reasonable time has elapsed.

(4) The tenant's judicial remedies under § 92.0563 shall be limited to recovery against the landlord to whom the tenant gave the required notices until the tenant has given the new landlord the notices required by this section and otherwise complied with § 92.056 as to the new landlord.

(5) If the new landlord violates this subsection, the new landlord is liable to the tenant for a civil penalty of one month's rent plus $2,000, actual damages, and attorney's fees.

(6) No provision of this section shall affect any right of a foreclosing superior lienholder to terminate, according to law, any interest in the premises held by the holders of subordinate liens, encumbrances, leases, or other interests and shall not affect any right of the tenant to terminate the lease according to law.

§ 92.0563 Tenant's judicial remedies

(a) A tenant's judicial remedies under § 92.056 shall include:

(1) an order directing the landlord to take reasonable action to repair or remedy the condition;

(2) an order reducing the tenant's rent, from the date of the first repair notice, in proportion to the reduced rental value resulting from the condition until the condition is repaired or remedied;

(3) a judgment against the landlord for a civil penalty of one month's rent plus $500;

(4) a judgment against the landlord for the amount of the tenant's actual damages; and

(5) court costs and attorney's fees, excluding any attorney's fees for a cause of action for damages relating to a personal injury.

(b) A landlord who knowingly violates § 92.006 by contracting orally or in writing with a tenant to waive the landlord's duty to repair under this subchapter shall be liable to the tenant for actual damages, a civil penalty of one month's rent plus $2,000, and reasonable attorney's fees. For purposes of this subsection, there shall be a rebuttable presumption that the landlord acted without knowledge of the violation. The tenant shall have the burden of pleading and proving a knowing violation. If the lease is in writing and is not in violation of § 92.006, the tenant's proof of a knowing violation must be clear and convincing. A mutual agreement for tenant repair under Subsection (g) of § 92.0561 is not a violation of § 92.006.

(c) The justice, county, and district courts have concurrent jurisdiction in an action under Subsection (a).

(d) If a suit is filed in a justice court requesting relief under Subsection (a), the justice court shall conduct a hearing on the request not earlier than the sixth day after the date of service of citation and not later than the 10th day after that date.

(e) A justice court may not award a judgment under this section, including an order of repair, that exceeds $10,000, excluding interest and costs of court.

(f) An appeal of a judgment of a justice court under this section takes precedence in county court and may be held at any time after the eighth day after the date the transcript is filed in the county court. An owner of real property who files a notice of appeal of a judgment of a justice court to the county court perfects the owner's appeal and stays the effect of the judgment without the necessity of posting an appeal bond.

§ 92.058 Landlord remedy for tenant violation

(a) If the tenant withholds rents, causes repairs to be performed, or makes rent deductions for repairs in violation of this subchapter, the landlord may recover actual damages from the tenant. If, after a landlord has notified a tenant in writing of (1) the illegality of the tenant's rent withholding or the tenant's proposed repair and (2) the penalties of this subchapter, the tenant withholds rent, causes repairs to be performed, or makes rent deductions for repairs in bad faith violation of this subchapter, the landlord may recover from the tenant a civil penalty of one month's rent plus $500.

(b) Notice under this section must be in writing and may be given in person, by mail, or by delivery to the premises.

(c) The landlord has the burden of pleading and proving, by clear and convincing evidence, that the landlord gave the tenant the required notice of the illegality and the penalties and that the tenant's violation was done in bad faith.   In any litigation under this subsection, the prevailing party shall recover reasonable attorney's fees from the non-prevailing party.

§ 92.060 Agents for delivery of notice
A managing agent, leasing agent, or resident manager is the agent of the landlord for purposes of notice and other communications required or permitted by this subchapter.

§ 92.061   Effect on other rights
The duties of a landlord and the remedies of a tenant under this subchapter are in lieu of existing common law and other statutory law warranties and duties of landlords for maintenance, repair, security, habitability, and nonretaliation, and remedies of tenants for a violation of those warranties and duties.   Otherwise, this subchapter does not affect any other right of a landlord or tenant under contract, statutory law, or common law that is consistent with the purposes of this subchapter or any right a landlord or tenant may have to bring an action for personal injury or property damage under the law of this state.   This subchapter does not impose obligations on a landlord or tenant other than those expressly stated in this subchapter.

§ 92.062 Lease term after natural disaster
If a rental premises is, as a practical matter, totally unusable for residential purposes as a result of a natural disaster such as a hurricane, tornado, flood, extended freeze, or widespread windstorm, a landlord that allows a tenant to move to another rental unit owned by the landlord may not require the tenant to execute a lease for a term longer than the term remaining on the tenant's lease on the date the premises was rendered unusable as a result of the natural disaster.

SUBCHAPTER C: SECURITY DEPOSITS

§ 92.101 Application
This subchapter applies to all residential leases.

§ 92.102 Security Deposit
A security deposit is any advance of money, other than a rental application deposit or an advance payment of rent, that is intended primarily to secure performance under a lease of a dwelling that has been entered into by a landlord and a tenant.

§ 92.103 Obligation to Refund
(a) Except as provided by § 92.107, the landlord shall refund a security deposit to the tenant on or before the 30th day after the date the tenant surrenders the premises.

(b) A requirement that a tenant give advance notice of surrender as a condition for refunding the security deposit is effective only if the requirement is underlined or is printed in conspicuous bold print in the lease.

(c) The tenant's claim to the security deposit takes priority over the claim of any creditor of the landlord, including a trustee in bankruptcy.

§ 92.103   Conditions for retention of security deposit or rent prepayment
(a) Except as provided in Subsection (b), a landlord who receives a security deposit or rent prepayment for a dwelling from a tenant who fails to occupy the dwelling according to a lease between the landlord and the tenant may not retain the security deposit or rent prepayment if:

(1) the tenant secures a replacement tenant satisfactory to the landlord and the replacement tenant occupies the dwelling on or before the commencement date of the lease; or

(2) the landlord secures a replacement tenant satisfactory to the landlord and the replacement tenant occupies the dwelling on or before the commencement date of the lease.

(b) If the landlord secures the replacement tenant, the landlord may retain and deduct from the security deposit or rent prepayment either:

(1) a sum agreed to in the lease as a lease cancellation fee;   or

(2) actual expenses incurred by the landlord in securing the replacement, including a reasonable amount for the time of the landlord in securing the replacement tenant.

§ 92.104 Retention of security deposit; accounting

(a) Before returning a security deposit, the landlord may deduct from the deposit damages and charges for which the tenant is legally liable under the lease or as a result of breaching the lease.

(b) The landlord may not retain any portion of a security deposit to cover normal wear and tear.

(c) If the landlord retains all or part of a security deposit under this section, the landlord shall give to the tenant the balance of the security deposit, if any, together with a written description and itemized list of all deductions.   The landlord is not required to give the tenant a description and itemized list of deductions if:

(1) the tenant owes rent when he surrenders possession of the premises;   and

(2) there is no controversy concerning the amount of rent owed.

§ 92.1041 Presumption of refund or accounting

A landlord is presumed to have refunded a security deposit or made an accounting of security deposit deductions if, on or before the date required under this subchapter, the refund or accounting is placed in the United States mail and postmarked on or before the required date.

§ 92.105 Cessation of owner's interest

(a) If the owner's interest in the premises is terminated by sale, assignment, death, appointment of a receiver, bankruptcy, or otherwise, the new owner is liable for the return of security deposits according to this subchapter from the date title to the premises is acquired, regardless of whether notice is given to the tenant under Subsection (b) of this section.

(b) The person who no longer owns an interest in the rental premises remains liable for a security deposit received while the person was the owner until the new owner delivers to the tenant a signed statement acknowledging that the new owner has received and is responsible for the tenant's security deposit and specifying the exact dollar amount of the deposit.

(c) Subsection (a) does not apply to a real estate mortgage lienholder who acquires title by foreclosure.

§ 92.106 Records
The landlord shall keep accurate records of all security deposits.

§ 92.107   Tenant's forwarding address
(a)   The landlord is not obligated to return a tenant's security deposit or give the tenant a written description of damages and charges until the tenant gives the landlord a written statement of the tenant's forwarding address for the purpose of refunding the security deposit.
(b) The tenant does not forfeit the right to a refund of the security deposit or the right to receive a description of damages and charges merely for failing to give a forwarding address to the landlord.

§ 92.108 Liability for Withholding Last Month Rent
(a) The tenant may not withhold payment of any portion of the last month's rent on grounds that the security deposit is security for unpaid rent.
(b) A tenant who violates this section is presumed to have acted in bad faith.   A tenant who in bad faith violates this section is liable to the landlord for an amount equal to three times the rent wrongfully withheld and the landlord's reasonable attorney's fees in a suit to recover the rent.

§ 92.109 Liability of landlord
(a) A landlord who in bad faith retains a security deposit in violation of this subchapter is liable for an amount equal to the sum of $100, three times the portion of the deposit wrongfully withheld, and the tenant's reasonable attorney's fees in a suit to recover the deposit.
(b) A landlord who in bad faith does not provide a written description and itemized list of damages and charges in violation of this subchapter:
(1) forfeits the right to withhold any portion of the security deposit or to bring suit against the tenant for damages to the premises; and
(2) is liable for the tenant's reasonable attorney's fees in a suit to recover the deposit.

(c) In an action brought by a tenant under this subchapter, the landlord has the burden of proving that the retention of any portion of the security deposit was reasonable.

(d) A landlord who fails either to return a security deposit or to provide a written description and itemization of deductions on or before the 30th day after the date the tenant surrenders possession is presumed to have acted in bad faith.

§ 92.110 Lease without security deposit; required notice

(a) If a security deposit was not required by a residential lease and the tenant is liable for damages and charges on surrender of the premises, the landlord shall notify the tenant in writing of the landlord's claim for damages and charges on or before the date the landlord reports the claim to a consumer reporting agency or third-party debt collector.

(b) A landlord is not required to provide the notice under Subsection (a) if the tenant has not given the landlord the tenant's forwarding address as provided by § 92.107.

(c) If a landlord does not provide the tenant the notice as required by this section, the landlord forfeits the right to collect damages and charges from the tenant. Forfeiture of the right to collect damages and charges from the tenant is the exclusive remedy for the failure to provide the proper notice to the tenant.

§ 92.111 Fee in lieu of security deposit

(a) If a security deposit is required by a residential lease, the landlord may choose to offer the tenant an option to pay a fee in lieu of a security deposit.   If a landlord offers a tenant the option of paying a fee in lieu of a security deposit, the landlord:

(1) shall offer the tenant the option to instead pay a security deposit; and

(2) may not use a prospective tenant's choice to pay a fee in lieu of a security deposit or a security deposit as a criterion in the determination of whether to approve an application for occupancy.

(b) At the time a landlord offers to a tenant the option of paying a fee in lieu of a security deposit, the landlord shall notify the tenant in writing:

(1) that the tenant has the option to instead pay a security deposit;

(2) that the tenant has the option to terminate the agreement to pay the fee in lieu of a security deposit at any time and stop paying the fee, and

instead, to pay a security deposit in the amount that is otherwise offered to new tenants for substantially similar housing on the date the tenant chooses to pay the security deposit; and

(3) of the charges for each option described by Subdivision (1) or (2).

(c) If the tenant decides to pay a fee in lieu of a security deposit, an agreement to collect the fee must be in writing and signed by:

(1) the landlord or the landlord's legal representative; and

(2) the tenant.

(d) A fee in lieu of a security deposit must be:

(1) a recurring fee of equivalent amount; and

(2) payable at the time each rent payment is due during the lease.

(e) A fee collected under this section may be used to purchase insurance coverage for damages and charges for which the tenant is legally liable under the lease or as a result of breaching the lease.   A landlord may not charge the tenant a fee that is more than the reasonable cost of obtaining and administering the insurance purchased under this subsection.

(f) If the tenant decides to pay a fee in lieu of a security deposit and the landlord purchases insurance coverage as described by Subsection (e), an agreement required under Subsection (c) must clearly specify the following terms:

(1) the fee is being paid only to secure occupancy without a requirement of paying a security deposit;

(2) the fee, unless otherwise specified, is not refundable;

(3) payment of the fee, unless otherwise specified, does not eliminate, release, or otherwise limit the requirements of the lease, including that the tenant must pay for:

(A) rent as the rent becomes due; and

(B) damages for which the tenant is legally liable under the lease, other than normal wear and tear; and

(4) the fee, unless otherwise specified, is not paying for insurance that covers the tenant or otherwise changes the tenant's obligation to pay rent and damages beyond normal wear and tear.

(g) Except as provided by Subsection (h), a fee collected under this section is a security deposit for purposes of this chapter.

(h) A fee collected under this section is not a security deposit for purposes of this chapter if:

(1) an agreement was signed under Subsection (c); and

(2) the fee is used to purchase insurance coverage for damages and unpaid rent for which the tenant is legally liable under the lease or as a result of breaching the lease.

(i) A landlord may not charge a tenant for normal wear and tear of a dwelling.

(j) A landlord may not submit a claim for damages or unpaid rent to an insurer for insurance described by Subsection (e) unless the landlord notifies the tenant of the damages or unpaid rent indebtedness not later than the 30th day after the date the tenant surrendered possession of the dwelling. The notice must include a written description and itemized list of all damages, if any, and of unpaid rent, if any, including the dates the rent payments were due.

(k) If the tenant challenges the claim for damages or unpaid rent and that challenge results in a determination by the landlord or by a court that the notice of indebtedness is incorrect, the indebtedness is void and the landlord may not file an insurance claim for insurance purchased under Subsection (e) in the amount of the voided indebtedness. If the landlord has already submitted to the insurer a claim for the voided indebtedness, the claim must be withdrawn. If the insurance company has already paid the landlord for the invalidated claim, the landlord shall return the payment.

(l) If an insurer compensates a landlord for a tenant's damages or unpaid rent under a valid claim:

(1) the landlord may not seek or collect reimbursement from the tenant of the amounts that the insurer paid to the landlord;

(2) the insurer that has paid a landlord after receipt of a claim filed by a landlord, if allowed by a subrogation clause in the insurance described by Subsection (e) and before the first anniversary of the termination of the tenant's occupancy, may seek reimbursement from the tenant of only the amounts paid to the landlord; and

(3) the tenant is entitled to any defenses to payment against the insurer as against the landlord.

(m) If an insurer seeks reimbursement under Subsection (l)(2), the insurer must include in the reimbursement demand:

(1) evidence of damages or unpaid rent that the landlord submitted to the insurer;

(2) evidence of damage repair costs that the landlord submitted to the insurer; and

(3) a copy of the settled claim that documents payments made by the insurer to the landlord.

SUBCHAPTER D: SECURITY DEVICES

§ 92.151 Definitions
   In this subchapter:
      (1) "Doorknob lock" means a lock in a doorknob, with the lock operated from the exterior by a key, card, or combination and from the interior without a key, card, or combination.
      (2) "Door viewer" means a permanently installed device in an exterior door that allows a person inside the dwelling to view a person outside the door.   The device must be:
         (A) a clear glass pane or one-way mirror;   or
         (B) a peephole having a barrel with a one-way lens of glass or other substance providing an angle view of not less than 160 degrees.
      (3) "Exterior door" means a door providing access from a dwelling interior to the exterior.   The term includes a door between a living area and a garage but does not include a sliding glass door or a screen door.
      (4) "French doors" means a set of two exterior doors in which each door is hinged and abuts the other door when closed.   The term includes double-hinged patio doors.
      (5) "Keyed dead bolt" means:
         (A) a door lock not in the doorknob that:
            (i) locks with a bolt into the doorjamb; and
            (ii) is operated from the exterior by a key, card, or combination and from the interior by a knob or lever without a key, card, or combination; or
         (B) a doorknob lock that contains a bolt with at least a one-inch throw.
      (6) "Keyless bolting device" means a door lock not in the doorknob that locks:
         (A) with a bolt into a strike plate screwed into the portion of the doorjamb surface that faces the edge of the door when the door is closed or into a metal doorjamb that serves as the strike plate, operable only by knob or lever from the door's interior and not in any manner from the door's exterior, and that is commonly known as a keyless dead bolt;
         (B) by a drop bolt system operated by placing a central metal plate over a metal doorjamb restraint that protrudes from the doorjamb and that is affixed to the doorjamb frame by means of three case-hardened screws at least three inches in length.   One-half of the central plate must overlap the interior surface of the door and the other half of the central plate

119

must overlap the doorjamb when the plate is placed over the doorjamb restraint. The drop bolt system must prevent the door from being opened unless the central plate is lifted off of the doorjamb restraint by a person who is on the interior side of the door. The term "keyless bolting device" does not include a chain latch, flip latch, surface-mounted slide bolt, mortise door bolt, surface-mounted barrel bolt, surface-mounted swing bar door guard, spring-loaded nightlatch, foot bolt, or other lock or latch; or

(C) by a metal bar or metal tube that is placed across the entire interior side of the door and secured in place at each end of the bar or tube by heavy-duty metal screw hooks. The screw hooks must be at least three inches in length and must be screwed into the door frame stud or wall stud on each side of the door. The bar or tube must be capable of being secured to both of the screw hooks and must be permanently attached in some way to the door frame stud or wall stud. When secured to the screw hooks, the bar or tube must prevent the door from being opened unless the bar or tube is removed by a person who is on the interior side of the door.

(7) "Landlord" means a dwelling owner, lessor, sublessor, management company, or managing agent, including an on-site manager.

(8) "Multiunit complex" means two or more dwellings in one or more buildings that are:

(A) under common ownership;

(B) managed by the same owner, agent, or management company; and

(C) located on the same lot or tract or adjacent lots or tracts of land.

(9) "Possession of a dwelling" means occupancy by a tenant under a lease, including occupancy until the time the tenant moves out or a writ of possession is issued by a court. The term does not include occupancy before the initial occupancy date authorized under a lease.

(10) "Rekey" means to change or alter a security device that is operated by a key, card, or combination so that a different key, card, or combination is necessary to operate the security device.

(11) "Security device" means a doorknob lock, door viewer, keyed dead bolt, keyless bolting device, sliding door handle latch, sliding door pin lock, sliding door security bar, or window latch in a dwelling.

(12) "Sliding door handle latch" means a latch or lock:

(A) located near the handle on a sliding glass door;

(B) operated with or without a key; and

(C) designed to prevent the door from being opened.

(13) "Sliding door pin lock" means a lock on a sliding glass door that consists of a pin or nail inserted from the interior side of the door at the side opposite the door's handle and that is designed to prevent the door from being opened or lifted.

(14) "Sliding door security bar" means a bar or rod that can be placed at the bottom of or across the interior side of the fixed panel of a sliding glass door and that is designed to prevent the door from being opened.

(15) "Tenant turnover date" means the date a tenant moves into a dwelling under a lease after all previous occupants have moved out. The term does not include dates of entry or occupation not authorized by the landlord.

(16) "Window latch" means a device on a window that prevents the window from being opened and that is operated without a key and only from the interior.

§ 92.152 Application of subchapter

(a) This subchapter does not apply to:

(1) a room in a hotel, motel, or inn or to similar transient housing;

(2) residential housing owned or operated by a public or private college or university accredited by a recognized accrediting agency as defined under § 61.003, Education Code;

(3) residential housing operated by preparatory schools accredited by the Texas Education Agency, a regional accrediting agency, or any accrediting agency recognized by the commissioner of education; or

(4) a temporary residential tenancy created by a contract for sale in which the buyer occupies the property before closing or the seller occupies the property after closing for a specific term not to exceed 90 days.

(b) Except as provided by Subsection (a), a dwelling to which this subchapter applies includes:

(1) a room in a dormitory or rooming house;

(2) a mobile home;

(3) a single family house, duplex, or triplex; and

(4) a living unit in an apartment, condominium, cooperative, or townhome project.

§ 92.153 Security devices required without necessity of tenant request

(a)   Except as provided by Subsections (b), (e), (f), (g), and (h) and without necessity of request by the tenant, a dwelling must be equipped with:

(1) a window latch on each exterior window of the dwelling;

(2) a doorknob lock or keyed dead bolt on each exterior door;

(3) a sliding door pin lock on each exterior sliding glass door of the dwelling;

(4) a sliding door handle latch or a sliding door security bar on each exterior sliding glass door of the dwelling; and

(5) a keyless bolting device and a door viewer on each exterior door of the dwelling.

(b) If the dwelling has French doors, one door of each pair of French doors must meet the requirements of Subsection (a) and the other door must have:

(1) a keyed dead bolt or keyless bolting device capable of insertion into the doorjamb above the door and a keyless bolting device capable of insertion into the floor or threshold, each with a bolt having a throw of one inch or more;   or

(2) a bolt installed inside the door and operated from the edge of the door, capable of insertion into the doorjamb above the door, and another bolt installed inside the door and operated from the edge of the door capable of insertion into the floor or threshold, each bolt having a throw of three-fourths inch or more.

(c) A security device required by Subsection (a) or (b) must be installed at the landlord's expense.

(d) Subsections (a) and (b) apply only when a tenant is in possession of a dwelling.

(e) A keyless bolting device is not required to be installed at the landlord's expense on an exterior door if:

(1) the dwelling is part of a multiunit complex in which the majority of dwelling units are leased to tenants who are over 55 years of age or who have a physical or mental disability;

(2) a tenant or occupant in the dwelling is over 55 years of age or has a physical or mental disability; and

(3) the landlord is expressly required or permitted to periodically check on the well-being or health of the tenant as a part of a written lease or other written agreement.

(f) A keyless bolting device is not required to be installed at the landlord's expense if a tenant or occupant in the dwelling is over 55 years of age or has a physical or mental disability, the tenant requests, in writing, that the landlord deactivate or not install the keyless bolting device, and the tenant certifies in the request that the tenant or occupant is over 55 years of age or has a physical or mental disability. The request must be a separate document and may not be included as part of a lease agreement. A landlord is not exempt as provided by this subsection if the landlord knows or has reason to know that the requirements of this subsection are not fulfilled.

(g) A keyed dead bolt or a doorknob lock is not required to be installed at the landlord's expense on an exterior door if at the time the tenant agrees to lease the dwelling:

(1) at least one exterior door usable for normal entry into the dwelling has both a keyed dead bolt and a keyless bolting device, installed in accordance with the height, strike plate, and throw requirements of § 92.154; and

(2) all other exterior doors have a keyless bolting device installed in accordance with the height, strike plate, and throw requirements of § 92.154.

(h) A security device required by this section must be operable throughout the time a tenant is in possession of a dwelling. However, a landlord may deactivate or remove the locking mechanism of a doorknob lock or remove any device not qualifying as a keyless bolting device if a keyed dead bolt has been installed on the same door.

(i) A landlord is subject to the tenant remedies provided by § 92.164(a)(4) if the landlord:

(1) deactivates or does not install a keyless bolting device, claiming an exemption under Subsection (e), (f), or (g); and

(2) knows or has reason to know that the requirements of the subsection granting the exemption are not fulfilled.

§ 92.154 Height, strike plate, and throw requirements--keyed dead bolt or keyless bolting device

(a) A keyed dead bolt or a keyless bolting device required by this subchapter must be installed at a height:

(1) not lower than 36 inches from the floor; and

(2) not higher than:

(A) 54 inches from the floor, if installed before September 1, 1993; or

(B) 48 inches from the floor, if installed on or after September 1, 1993.

(b) A keyed dead bolt or a keyless bolting device described in §
92.151(6)(A) or (B) in a dwelling must:
    (1) have a strike plate screwed into the portion of the doorjamb surface
that faces the edge of the door when the door is closed; or
    (2) be installed in a door with a metal doorjamb that serves as the
strike plate.
    (c) A keyed dead bolt or keyless dead bolt, as described by Section
92.151(6)(A), installed in a dwelling on or after September 1, 1993, must
have a bolt with a throw of not less than one inch.
    (d) The requirements of this section do not apply to a keyed dead bolt or a
keyless bolting device in one door of a pair of French doors that is installed in
accordance with the requirements of Section 92.153(b)(1) or (2).

§ 92.155 Height requirements--sliding door security devices
    A sliding door pin lock or sliding door security bar required by this
subchapter must be installed at a height not higher than:
    (1) 54 inches from the floor, if installed before September 1, 1993; or
    (2) 48 inches from the floor, if installed on or after September 1, 1993.

§ 92.156 Rekeying or change of security devices
    (a) A security device operated by a key, card, or combination shall be
rekeyed by the landlord at the landlord's expense not later than the seventh
day after each tenant turnover date.
    (b) A landlord shall perform additional rekeying or change a security
device at the tenant's expense if requested by the tenant.   A tenant may
make an unlimited number of requests under this subsection.
    (c) The expense of rekeying security devices for purposes of the use or
change of the landlord's master key must be paid by the landlord.
    (d) This section does not apply to locks on closet doors or other interior
doors.

§ 92.157 Security devices requested by tenant
    (a) At a tenant's request made at any time, a landlord, at the tenant's
expense, shall install:
    (1) a keyed dead bolt on an exterior door if the door has:
        (A) a doorknob lock but not a keyed dead bolt; or

(B) a keyless bolting device but not a keyed dead bolt or doorknob lock; and

(2) a sliding door pin lock or sliding door security bar if the door is an exterior sliding glass door without a sliding door pin lock or sliding door security bar.

(b) At a tenant's request made before January 1, 1995, a landlord, at the tenant's expense, shall install on an exterior door of a dwelling constructed before September 1, 1993:

(1) a keyless bolting device if the door does not have a keyless bolting device; and

(2) a door viewer if the door does not have a door viewer.

(c) If a security device required by § 92.153 to be installed on or after January 1, 1995, without necessity of a tenant's request has not been installed by the landlord, the tenant may request the landlord to immediately install it, and the landlord shall immediately install it at the landlord's expense.

§ 92.158 Landlord's duty to repair or replace security device

During the lease term and any renewal period, a landlord shall repair or replace a security device on request or notification by the tenant that the security device is inoperable or in need of repair or replacement.

§ 92.159 When tenant's request or notice must be in writing

A tenant's request or notice under this subchapter may be given orally unless the tenant has a written lease that requires the request or notice to be in writing and that requirement is underlined or in boldfaced print in the lease.

§ 92.160 Type, brand, and manner of installation

Except as otherwise required by this subchapter, a landlord may select the type, brand, and manner of installation, including placement, of a security device installed under this subchapter.   This section does not apply to a security device installed, repaired, changed, replaced, or rekeyed by a tenant under § 92.164(a)(1) or § 92.165(1).

§ 92.161 Compliance with tenant request required within reasonable time

(a) Except as provided by Subsections (b) and (c), a landlord must comply with a tenant's request for rekeying, changing, installing, repairing, or replacing a security device under § 92.156, 92.157, or 92.158 within a reasonable time. A reasonable time for purposes of this subsection is presumed to be not later than the seventh day after the date the request is received by the landlord.

(b) If within the time allowed under Section 92.162(c) a landlord requests advance payment of charges that the landlord is entitled to collect under that section, the landlord shall comply with a tenant's request under § 92.156(b), 92.157(a), or 92.157(b) within a reasonable time. A reasonable time for purposes of this subsection is presumed to be not later than the seventh day after the date a tenant's advance payment is received by the landlord, except as provided by Subsection (c).

(c) A reasonable time for purposes of Subsections (a) and (b) is presumed to be not later than 72 hours after the time of receipt of the tenant's request and any required advance payment if at the time of making the request the tenant informed the landlord that:

(1) an unauthorized entry occurred or was attempted in the tenant's dwelling;

(2) an unauthorized entry occurred or was attempted in another unit in the multiunit complex in which the tenant's dwelling is located during the two months preceding the date of the request; or

(3) a crime of personal violence occurred in the multiunit complex in which the tenant's dwelling is located during the two months preceding the date of the request.

(d) A landlord may rebut the presumption provided by Subsection (a) or (b) if despite the diligence of the landlord:

(1) the landlord did not know of the tenant's request, without the fault of the landlord;

(2) materials, labor, or utilities were unavailable; or

(3) a delay was caused by circumstances beyond the landlord's control, including the illness or death of the landlord or a member of the landlord's immediate family.

(e) This section does not apply to a landlord's duty to install or rekey, without necessity of a tenant's request, a security device under § 92.153 or 92.156(a).

§ 92.162 Payment of charges; limits on amount charged

(a) A landlord may not require a tenant to pay for repair or replacement of a security device due to normal wear and tear. A landlord may not require a tenant to pay for other repairs or replacements of a security device except as provided by Subsections (b), (c), and (d).

(b) A landlord may require a tenant to pay for repair or replacement of a security device if an underlined provision in a written lease authorizes the landlord to do so and the repair or replacement is necessitated by misuse or damage by the tenant, a member of the tenant's family, an occupant, or a guest, and not by normal wear and tear. Misuse of or damage to a security device that occurs during the tenant's occupancy is presumed to be caused by the tenant, a family member, an occupant, or a guest. The tenant has the burden of proving that the misuse or damage was caused by another party.

(c) A landlord may require a tenant to pay in advance charges for which the tenant is liable under this subchapter if a written lease authorizes the landlord to require advance payment, and the landlord notifies the tenant within a reasonable time after the tenant's request that advance payment is required, and:

(1) the tenant is more than 30 days delinquent in reimbursing the landlord for charges to which the landlord is entitled under Subsection (b); or

(2) the tenant requested that the landlord repair, install, change, or rekey the same security device during the 30 days preceding the tenant's request, and the landlord complied with the request.

(d) A landlord authorized by this subchapter to charge a tenant for repairing, installing, changing, or rekeying a security device under this subchapter may not require the tenant to pay more than the total cost charged by a third-party contractor for material, labor, taxes, and extra keys. If the landlord's employees perform the work, the charge may include a reasonable amount for overhead but may not include a profit to the landlord. If management company employees perform the work, the charge may include reasonable overhead and profit but may not exceed the cost charged to the owner by the management company for comparable security devices installed by management company employees at the owner's request and expense.

(e) The owner of a dwelling shall reimburse a management company, managing agent, or on-site manager for costs expended by that person in complying with this subchapter. A management company, managing agent, or on-site manager may reimburse itself for the costs from the owner's funds in its possession or control.

§ 92.163 Removal or alteration of security device by tenant
A security device that is installed, changed, or rekeyed under this subchapter becomes a fixture of the dwelling. Except as provided by § 92.164(a)(1) or 92.165(1) regarding the remedy of repair-and-deduct, a tenant may not remove, change, rekey, replace, or alter a security device or have it removed, changed, rekeyed, replaced, or altered without permission of the landlord.

§ 92.164 Tenant remedies for landlord's failure to install or rekey certain security devices
(a) If a landlord does not comply with § 92.153 or 92.156(a) regarding installation or rekeying of a security device, the tenant may:
(1) install or rekey the security device as required by this subchapter and deduct the reasonable cost of material, labor, taxes, and extra keys from the tenant's next rent payment, in accordance with § 92.166;
(2) serve a written request for compliance on the landlord, and, except as provided by Subsections (b) and (c), if the landlord does not comply on or before the third day after the date the notice is received, unilaterally terminate the lease without court proceedings;
(3) file suit against the landlord without serving a request for compliance and obtain a judgment for:
(A) a court order directing the landlord to comply, if the tenant is in possession of the dwelling;
(B) the tenant's actual damages;
(C) court costs; and
(D) attorney's fees except in suits for recovery of property damages, personal injuries, or wrongful death; and
(4) serve a written request for compliance on the landlord, and, except as provided by Subsections (b) and (c), if the landlord does not comply on or before the third day after the date the notice is received, file suit against the landlord and obtain a judgment for:
(A) a court order directing the landlord to comply and bring all dwellings owned by the landlord into compliance, if the tenant serving the written request is in possession of the dwelling;
(B) the tenant's actual damages;
(C) punitive damages if the tenant suffers actual damages;
(D) a civil penalty of one month's rent plus $500;
(E) court costs; and

    (F) attorney's fees except in suits for recovery of property damages, personal injuries, or wrongful death.

    (b) A tenant may not unilaterally terminate the lease under Subsection (a)(2) or file suit against the landlord to obtain a judgment under Subsection (a)(4) unless the landlord does not comply on or before the seventh day after the date the written request for compliance is received if the lease includes language underlined or in boldface print that in substance provides the tenant with notice that:

    (1) the landlord at the landlord's expense is required to equip the dwelling, when the tenant takes possession, with the security devices described by §§ 92.153(a)(1)-(4) and (6);

    (2) the landlord is not required to install a doorknob lock or keyed dead bolt at the landlord's expense if the exterior doors meet the requirements of § 92.153(f);

    (3) the landlord is not required to install a keyless bolting device at the landlord's expense on an exterior door if the landlord is expressly required or permitted to periodically check on the well-being or health of the tenant as provided by § 92.153(e)(3); and

    (4) the tenant has the right to install or rekey a security device required by this subchapter and deduct the reasonable cost from the tenant's next rent payment, as provided by Subsection (a)(1).

    (c) Regardless of whether the lease contains language complying with the requirements of Subsection (b), the additional time for landlord compliance provided by Subsection (b) does not apply if at the time the tenant served the written request for compliance on the landlord the tenant informed the landlord that an unauthorized entry occurred or was attempted in the tenant's dwelling, an unauthorized entry occurred or was attempted in another unit in the multiunit complex in which the tenant's dwelling is located during the two months preceding the date of the request, or a crime of personal violence occurred in the multiunit complex in which the tenant's dwelling is located during the two months preceding the date of the request, unless despite the diligence of the landlord:

    (1) the landlord did not know of the tenant's request, without the fault of the landlord;

    (2) materials, labor, or utilities were unavailable; or

    (3) a delay was caused by circumstances beyond the landlord's control, including the illness or death of the landlord or a member of the landlord's immediate family.

§ 92.1641 Landlord's defenses relating to installing or rekeying certain security devices

The landlord has a defense to liability under § 92.164 if:

(1) the tenant has not fully paid all rent then due from the tenant on the date the tenant gives a request under Subsection (a) of § 92.157 or the notice required by § 92.164; or

(2) on the date the tenant terminates the lease or files suit the tenant has not fully paid costs requested by the landlord and authorized by § 92.162.

§ 92.165   Tenant remedies for other landlord violations

If a landlord does not comply with a tenant's request regarding rekeying, changing, adding, repairing, or replacing a security device under § 92.156(b), 92.157, or 92.158 in accordance with the time limits and other requirements of this subchapter, the tenant may:

(1) install, repair, change, replace, or rekey the security devices as required by this subchapter and deduct the reasonable cost of material, labor, taxes, and extra keys from the tenant's next rent payment in accordance with § 92.166;

(2) unilaterally terminate the lease without court proceedings;   and

(3) file suit against the landlord and obtain a judgment for:

(A) a court order directing the landlord to comply, if the tenant is in possession of the dwelling;

(B) the tenant's actual damages;

(C) punitive damages if the tenant suffers actual damages and the landlord's failure to comply is intentional, malicious, or grossly negligent;

(D) a civil penalty of one month's rent plus $500;

(E) court costs; and

(F) attorney's fees except in suits for recovery of property damages, personal injuries, or wrongful death.

§ 92.166   Notice of tenant's deduction of repair costs from rent

(a) A tenant shall notify the landlord of a rent deduction attributable to the tenant's installing, repairing, changing, replacing, or rekeying of a security device under § 92.164(a)(1) or 92.165(1) after the landlord's failure to comply with this subchapter.   The notice must be given at the time of the reduced rent payment.

(b) Unless otherwise provided in a written lease, a tenant shall provide one duplicate of the key to any key-operated security device installed or rekeyed by the tenant under Section 92.164(a)(1) or 92.165(1) within a reasonable time after the landlord's written request for the key.

§ 92.167 Landlord's defenses relating to compliance with tenant's request

(a) A landlord has a defense to liability under § 92.165 if on the date the tenant terminates the lease or files suit the tenant has not fully paid costs requested by the landlord and authorized by this subchapter.

(b) A management company or managing agent who is not the owner of a dwelling and who has not purported to be the owner in the lease has a defense to liability under §§ 92.164 and 92.165 if before the date the tenant is in possession of the dwelling or the date of the tenant's request for installation, repair, replacement, change, or rekeying and before any property damage or personal injury to the tenant, the management company or managing agent:

(1) did not have funds of the dwelling owner in its possession or control with which to comply with this subchapter;

(2) made written request to the dwelling owner that the owner fund and allow installation, repair, change, replacement, or rekeying of security devices as required under this subchapter and mailed the request, certified mail return receipt requested, to the dwelling owner;   and

(3) not later than the third day after the date of receipt of the tenant's request, provided the tenant with a written notice:

(A) stating that the management company or managing agent has taken the actions in Subdivisions (1) and (2);

(B) stating that the owner has not provided or will not provide the necessary funds;   and

(C) explaining the remedies available to the tenant for the landlord's failure to comply.

§ 92.168 Tenant's remedy on notice from management company

The tenant may unilaterally terminate the lease or exercise other remedies under §§ 92.164 and 92.165 after receiving written notice from a management company that the owner of the dwelling has not provided or will not provide funds to repair, install, change, replace, or rekey a security device as required by this subchapter.

§ 92.169   Agent for delivery of notice

A managing agent or an agent to whom rent is regularly paid, whether residing or maintaining an office on-site or off-site, is the agent of the landlord for purposes of notice and other communications required or permitted by this subchapter.

§ 92.170   Effect on other landlord duties and tenant remedies

The duties of a landlord and the remedies of a tenant under this subchapter are in lieu of common law, other statutory law, and local ordinances relating to a residential landlord's duty to install, change, rekey, repair, or replace security devices and a tenant's remedies for the landlord's failure to install, change, rekey, repair, or replace security devices, except that a municipal ordinance adopted before January 1, 1993, may require installation of security devices at the landlord's expense by an earlier date than a date required by this subchapter.   This subchapter does not affect a duty of a landlord or a remedy of a tenant under Subchapter B regarding habitability.

SUBCHAPTER E. DISCLOSURE OF OWNERSHIP AND MANAGEMENT

§ 92.201 Disclosure of ownership and management

(a) A landlord shall disclose to a tenant, or to any government official or employee acting in an official capacity, according to this subchapter:

(1) the name and either a street or post office box address of the holder of record title, according to the deed records in the county clerk's office, of the dwelling rented by the tenant or inquired about by the government official or employee acting in an official capacity;   and

(2) if an entity located off-site from the dwelling is primarily responsible for managing the dwelling, the name and street address of the management company.

(b) Disclosure to a tenant under Subsection (a) must be made by:

(1) giving the information in writing to the tenant on or before the seventh day after the day the landlord receives the tenant's request for the information;

(2) continuously posting the information in a conspicuous place in the dwelling or the office of the on-site manager or on the outside of the entry door to the office of the on-site manager on or before the seventh day after the date the landlord receives the tenant's request for the information; or

(3) including the information in a copy of the tenant's lease or in written rules given to the tenant before the tenant requests the information.

(c) Disclosure of information to a tenant may be made under Subdivision (1) or (2) of Subsection (b) before the tenant requests the information.

(d) Disclosure of information to a government official or employee must be made by giving the information in writing to the official or employee on or before the seventh day after the date the landlord receives the request from the official or employee for the information.

(e) A correction to the information may be made by any of the methods authorized for providing the information.

(f) For the purposes of this section, an owner or property manager may disclose either an actual name or names or an assumed name if an assumed name certificate has been recorded with the county clerk.

§ 92.202 Landlord's failure to disclose information

(a) A landlord is liable to a tenant or a governmental body according to this subchapter if:

(1) after the tenant or government official or employee makes a request for information under § 92.201, the landlord does not provide the information; and

(2) the landlord does not give the information to the tenant or government official or employee before the eighth day after the date the tenant, official, or employee gives the landlord written notice that the tenant, official, or employee may exercise remedies under this subchapter if the landlord does not comply with the request by the tenant, official, or employee for the information within seven days.

(b) If the tenant's lease is in writing, the lease may require the tenant's initial request for information to be written. A request by a government official or employee for information must be in writing.

§ 92.203 Landlord's failure to correct information

A landlord who has provided information under Subdivision (2) or (3) of Subsection (b) of Section 92.201 is liable to a tenant according to this subchapter if:

(1) the information becomes incorrect because a name or address changes; and

(2) the landlord fails to correct the information on or before the seventh day after the date the tenant gives the landlord written notice that the tenant may exercise the remedies under this subchapter if the corrected information is not provided within seven days.

§ 92.204 Bad faith violation

A landlord acts in bad faith and is liable according to this subchapter if the landlord gives an incorrect name or address under Subsection (a) of Section 92.201 by willfully:

(1) disclosing incorrect information under Section 92.201(b)(1) or (2) or Section 92.201(d); or

(2) failing to correct information given under Section 92.201(b)(1) or (2) or Section 92.201(d) that the landlord knows is incorrect.

§ 92.205 Remedies

(a) A tenant of a landlord who is liable under § 92.202, 92.203, or 92.204 may obtain or exercise one or more of the following remedies:

(1) a court order directing the landlord to make a disclosure required by this subchapter;

(2) a judgment against the landlord for an amount equal to the tenant's actual costs in discovering the information required to be disclosed by this subchapter;

(3) a judgment against the landlord for one month's rent plus $100;

(4) a judgment against the landlord for court costs and attorney's fees; and

(5) unilateral termination of the lease without a court proceeding.

(b) A governmental body whose official or employee has requested information from a landlord who is liable under Section 92.202 or 92.204 may obtain or exercise one or more of the following remedies:

(1) a court order directing the landlord to make a disclosure required by this subchapter;

(2) a judgment against the landlord for an amount equal to the governmental body's actual costs in discovering the information required to be disclosed by this subchapter;

(3) a judgment against the landlord for $500; and

(4) a judgment against the landlord for court costs and attorney's fees.

§ 92.206 Landlord's defense

A landlord has a defense to liability under § 92.202 or 92.203 if the tenant owes rent on the date the tenant gives a notice required by either of those sections. Rent delinquency is not a defense for a violation of § 92.204.

§ 92.207 Agents for delivery of notice

(a) A managing or leasing agent, whether residing or maintaining an office on-site or off-site, is the agent of the landlord for purposes of:

(1) notice and other communications required or permitted by this subchapter;

(2) notice and other communications from a governmental body relating to a violation of health, sanitation, safety, or nuisance laws on the landlord's property where the dwelling is located, including notices of:

(A) demands for abatement of nuisances;

(B) repair of a substandard dwelling;

(C) remedy of dangerous conditions;

(D) reimbursement of costs incurred by the governmental body in curing the violation;

(E) fines; and

135

(F) service of process.

(b) If the landlord's name and business street address in this state have not been furnished in writing to the tenant or government official or employee, the person who collects the rent from a tenant is the landlord's authorized agent for purposes of Subsection (a).

§ 92.208   Additional enforcement by local ordinance

The duties of a landlord and the remedies of a tenant under this subchapter are in lieu of the common law, other statutory law, and local ordinances relating to the disclosure of ownership and management of a dwelling by a landlord to a tenant.   However, this subchapter does not prohibit the adoption of a local ordinance that conforms to this subchapter but which contains additional enforcement provisions.

SUBCHAPTER F. SMOKE ALARMS AND FIRE EXTINGUISHERS

§ 92.251 Definitions
In this subchapter:
(1) "Bedroom" means a room designed with the intent that it be used for sleeping purposes.
(2) "Dwelling unit" means a home, mobile home, duplex unit, apartment unit, condominium unit, or any dwelling unit in a multiunit residential structure. It also means a "dwelling" as defined by § 92.001.
(3) "Smoke alarm" means a device designed to detect and to alert occupants of a dwelling unit to the visible and invisible products of combustion by means of an audible alarm.

§ 92.252 Application of other law; municipal regulation
(a) The duties of a landlord and the remedies of a tenant under this subchapter are in lieu of common law, other statutory law, and local ordinances regarding a residential landlord's duty to install, inspect, or repair a fire extinguisher or smoke alarm in a dwelling unit. However, this subchapter does not:
(1) affect a local ordinance adopted before September 1, 1981, that requires landlords to install smoke alarms in new or remodeled dwelling units before September 1, 1981, if the ordinance conforms with or is amended to conform with this subchapter;
(2) limit or prevent adoption or enforcement of a local ordinance relating to fire safety as a part of a building, fire, or housing code, including any requirements relating to the installation of smoke alarms or the type of smoke alarms;
(3) otherwise limit or prevent the adoption of a local ordinance that conforms to this subchapter but which contains additional enforcement provisions, except as provided by Subsection (b); or
(4) affect a local ordinance that requires regular inspections by local officials of smoke alarms in dwelling units and that requires smoke alarms to be operational at the time of inspection.
(b) If a smoke alarm powered by battery has been installed in a dwelling unit built before September 1, 1987, in compliance with this subchapter and local ordinances, a local ordinance may not require that a smoke alarm powered by alternating current be installed in the unit unless:

(1) the interior of the unit is repaired, remodeled, or rebuilt at a projected cost of more than $5,000 and:

(A) the repair, remodeling, or rebuilding requires a municipal building permit; and

(B) either:

(i) the repair, remodeling, or rebuilding results in the removal of interior walls or ceiling finishes exposing the structure; or

(ii) the interior of the unit provides access for building wiring through an attic, crawl space, or basement without the removal of interior walls or ceiling finishes;

(2) an addition occurs to the unit at a projected cost of more than $5,000;

(3) a smoke alarm powered by alternating current was actually installed in the unit at any time prior to September 1, 1987; or

(4) a smoke alarm powered by alternating current was required by lawful city ordinance at the time of initial construction of the unit.

§ 92.253 Exemptions

(a) This subchapter does not apply to:

(1) a dwelling unit that is occupied by its owner, no part of which is leased to a tenant;

(2) a dwelling unit in a building five or more stories in height in which smoke alarms are required or regulated by local ordinance; or

(3) a nursing or convalescent home licensed by the Department of State Health Services and certified to meet the Life Safety Code under federal law and regulations.

(b) Notwithstanding this subchapter, a person licensed to install fire alarms or fire detection devices under Chapter 6002, Insurance Code, shall comply with that chapter when installing smoke alarms.

§ 92.254 Smoke alarm

(a) A smoke alarm must be:

(1) designed to detect both the visible and invisible products of combustion;

(2) designed with an alarm audible to a person in the bedrooms it serves; and

(3) tested and listed for use as a smoke alarm by Underwriters Laboratories, Inc., Factory Mutual Research Corporation, or United States Testing Company, Inc.

(a-1) If requested by a tenant as an accommodation for a person with a hearing-impairment disability or as required by law as a reasonable accommodation for a person with a hearing-impairment disability, a smoke alarm must, in addition to complying with Subsection (a), be capable of alerting a hearing-impaired person in the bedrooms it serves.

(b) Except as provided by § 92.255(b), a smoke alarm may be powered by battery, alternating current, or other power source as required by local ordinance. The power system and installation procedure of a security device that is electrically operated rather than battery operated must comply with applicable local ordinances.

§ 92.255 Installation and location

(a) A landlord shall install at least one smoke alarm in each separate bedroom in a dwelling unit. In addition:

(1) if the dwelling unit is designed to use a single room for dining, living, and sleeping, the smoke alarm must be located inside the room;

(2) if multiple bedrooms are served by the same corridor, at least one smoke alarm must be installed in the corridor in the immediate vicinity of the bedrooms; and

(3) if the dwelling unit has multiple levels, at least one smoke alarm must be located on each level.

(b) If a dwelling unit was occupied as a residence before September 1, 2011, or a certificate of occupancy was issued for the dwelling unit before that date, a smoke alarm installed in accordance with Subsection (a) may be powered by battery and is not required to be interconnected with other smoke alarms, except that a smoke alarm that is installed to replace a smoke alarm that was in place on the date the dwelling unit was first occupied as a residence must comply with residential building code standards that applied to the dwelling unit on that date or § 92.252(b).

§ 92.257 Installation procedure

(a) Subject to Subsections (b) and (c), a smoke alarm must be installed according to the manufacturer's recommended procedures.

(b) A smoke alarm must be installed on a ceiling or wall. If on a ceiling, it must be no closer than six inches to a wall or otherwise located in accordance with the manufacturer's installation instructions. If on a wall, it must be no closer than six inches and no farther than 12 inches from the ceiling or otherwise located in accordance with the manufacturer's installation instructions.

(c) A smoke alarm may be located other than as required by Subsection (a) or (b) if a local ordinance or a local or state fire marshal approves.

§ 92.2571 Alternative compliance

A landlord complies with the requirements of this subchapter relating to the provision of smoke alarms in the dwelling unit if the landlord:

(1) has a fire detection device, as defined by § 6002.002, Insurance Code, that includes a fire alarm device, as defined by § 6002.002, Insurance Code, installed in a dwelling unit; or

(2) for a dwelling unit that is a one-family or two-family dwelling unit, installs smoke detectors in compliance with Chapter 766, Health and Safety Code.

§ 92.258 Inspection and repair

(a) The landlord shall inspect and repair a smoke alarm according to this section.

(b) The landlord shall determine that the smoke alarm is in good working order at the beginning of the tenant's possession by testing the smoke alarm with smoke, by operating the testing button on the smoke alarm, or by following other recommended test procedures of the manufacturer for the particular model.

(c) During the term of a lease or during a renewal or extension, the landlord has a duty to inspect and repair a smoke alarm, but only if the tenant gives the landlord notice of a malfunction or requests to the landlord that the smoke alarm be inspected or repaired. This duty does not exist with respect to damage or a malfunction caused by the tenant, the tenant's family, or the tenant's guests or invitees during the term of the lease or a renewal or extension, except that the landlord has a duty to repair or replace the smoke alarm if the tenant pays in advance the reasonable repair or replacement cost, including labor, materials, taxes, and overhead.

(d) The landlord must comply with the tenant's request for inspection or repair of a smoke alarm within a reasonable time, considering the availability of material, labor, and utilities.

(e) The landlord has met the duty to inspect and repair if the smoke alarm is in good working order after the landlord tests the smoke alarm with smoke, operates the testing button on the smoke alarm, or follows other recommended test procedures of the manufacturer for the particular model.

(f) The landlord is not obligated to provide batteries for a battery-operated smoke alarm after a tenant takes possession if the smoke alarm was in good working order at the time the tenant took possession.

(g) A smoke alarm that is in good working order at the beginning of a tenant's possession is presumed to be in good working order until the tenant requests repair of the smoke alarm as provided by this subchapter.

§ 92.259   Landlord's failure to install, inspect, or repair

(a) A landlord is liable according to this subchapter if:

(1) the landlord did not install a smoke alarm at the time of initial occupancy by the tenant as required by this subchapter or a municipal ordinance permitted by this subchapter; or

(2) the landlord does not install, inspect, or repair the smoke alarm on or before the seventh day after the date the tenant gives the landlord written notice that the tenant may exercise his remedies under this subchapter if the landlord does not comply with the request within seven days.

(b) If the tenant gives notice under Subsection (a)(2) and the tenant's lease is in writing, the lease may require the tenant to make the initial request for installation, inspection, or repair of a smoke alarm in writing.

§ 92.260 Tenant remedies

A tenant of a landlord who is liable under Section 92.259 may obtain or exercise one or more of the following remedies:

(1) a court order directing the landlord to comply with the tenant's request if the tenant is in possession of the dwelling unit;

(2) a judgment against the landlord for damages suffered by the tenant because of the landlord's violation;

(3) a judgment against the landlord for a civil penalty of one month's rent plus $100 if the landlord violates Section 92.259(a)(2);

(4) a judgment against the landlord for court costs;

(5) a judgment against the landlord for attorney's fees in an action under Subdivision (1) or (3); and

(6) unilateral termination of the lease without a court proceeding if the landlord violates Section 92.259(a)(2).

§ 92.261 Landlord's defenses

The landlord has a defense to liability under § 92.259 if:

(1) on the date the tenant gives the notice required by § 92.259 the tenant has not paid all rent due from the tenant; or

(2) on the date the tenant terminates the lease or files suit the tenant has not fully paid costs requested by the landlord and authorized by § 92.258.

§ 92.2611 Tenant's disabling of a smoke alarm

(a) A tenant is liable according to this subchapter if the tenant removes a battery from a smoke alarm without immediately replacing it with a working battery or knowingly disconnects or intentionally damages a smoke alarm, causing it to malfunction.

(b) Except as provided in Subsection (c), a landlord of a tenant who is liable under Subsection (a) may obtain a judgment against the tenant for damages suffered by the landlord because the tenant removed a battery from a smoke alarm without immediately replacing it with a working battery or knowingly disconnected or intentionally damaged the smoke alarm, causing it to malfunction.

(c) A tenant is not liable for damages suffered by the landlord if the damage is caused by the landlord's failure to repair the smoke alarm within a reasonable time after the tenant requests it to be repaired, considering the availability of material, labor, and utilities.

(d) A landlord of a tenant who is liable under Subsection (a) may obtain or exercise one or more of the remedies in Subsection (e) if:

(1) a lease between the landlord and tenant contains a notice, in underlined or boldfaced print, which states in substance that the tenant must not disconnect or intentionally damage a smoke alarm or remove the battery without immediately replacing it with a working battery and that the tenant may be subject to damages, civil penalties, and attorney's fees under § 92.2611 of the Property Code for not complying with the notice; and

(2) the landlord has given notice to the tenant that the landlord intends to exercise the landlord's remedies under this subchapter if the tenant does not reconnect, repair, or replace the smoke alarm or replace the removed battery within seven days after being notified by the landlord to do so.

(d-1) The notice in Subsection (d)(2) must be in a separate document furnished to the tenant after the landlord has discovered that the tenant has disconnected or damaged the smoke alarm or removed a battery from it.

(e) If a tenant is liable under Subsection (a) and the tenant does not comply with the landlord's notice under Subsection (d), the landlord shall have the following remedies against the tenant:

(1) a court order directing the tenant to comply with the landlord's notice;

(2) a judgment against the tenant for a civil penalty of one month's rent plus $100;

(3) a judgment against the tenant for court costs;   and

(4) a judgment against the tenant for reasonable attorney's fees.

(f) A tenant's guest or invitee who suffers damage because of a landlord's failure to install, inspect, or repair a smoke alarm as required by this subchapter may recover a judgment against the landlord for the damage. A tenant's guest or invitee who suffers damage because the tenant removed a battery without immediately replacing it with a working battery or because the tenant knowingly disconnected or intentionally damaged the smoke alarm, causing it to malfunction, may recover a judgment against the tenant for the damage.

§ 92.262 Agents for delivery of notice

A managing or leasing agent, whether residing or maintaining an office on-site or off-site, is the agent of the landlord for purposes of notice and other communications required or permitted by this subchapter.

§ 92.263 Inspection of residential fire extinguisher

(a) If a landlord has installed a 1A10BC residential fire extinguisher as defined by the National Fire Protection Association or other non-rechargeable fire extinguisher in accordance with a local ordinance or other law, the landlord or the landlord's agent shall inspect the fire extinguisher:

(1) at the beginning of a tenant's possession; and

(2) within a reasonable time after receiving a written request by a tenant.

(b) At a minimum, an inspection under this section must include:

(1) checking to ensure the fire extinguisher is present; and

(2) checking to ensure the fire extinguisher gauge or pressure indicator indicates the correct pressure as recommended by the manufacturer of the fire extinguisher.

(c) A fire extinguisher that satisfies the inspection requirements of Subsection (b) at the beginning of a tenant's possession is presumed to be in good working order until the tenant requests an inspection in writing.

§ 92.264 Duty to repair or replace

(a) The landlord shall repair or replace a fire extinguisher at the landlord's expense if:

(1) on inspection, the fire extinguisher is found:

(A) not to be functioning; or

(B) not to have the correct pressure indicated on the gauge or pressure indicator as recommended by the manufacturer of the fire extinguisher; or

(2) a tenant has notified the landlord that the tenant has used the fire extinguisher for a legitimate purpose.

(b) If the tenant or the tenant's invited guest removes, misuses, damages, or otherwise disables a fire extinguisher:

(1) the landlord is not required to repair or replace the fire extinguisher at the landlord's expense; and

(2) the landlord is required to repair or replace the fire extinguisher within a reasonable time if the tenant pays in advance the reasonable repair or replacement cost, including labor, materials, taxes, and overhead.

SUBCHAPTER G. UTILITY CUTOFF

§ 92.301 Landlord Liability to Tenant for Utility Cutoff

(a) A landlord who has expressly or impliedly agreed in the lease to furnish and pay for water, gas, or electric service to the tenant's dwelling is liable to the tenant if the utility company has cut off utility service to the tenant's dwelling or has given written notice to the tenant that such utility service is about to be cut off because of the landlord's nonpayment of the utility bill.

(b) If a landlord is liable to the tenant under Subsection (a) of this section, the tenant may:

(1) pay the utility company money to reconnect or avert the cutoff of utilities according to this section;

(2) terminate the lease if the termination notice is in writing and move-out is to be within 30 days from the date the tenant has notice from the utility company of a future cutoff or notice of an actual cutoff, whichever is sooner;

(3) deduct from the tenant's rent, without necessity of judicial action, the amounts paid to the utility company to reconnect or avert a cutoff;

(4) if the lease is terminated by the tenant, deduct the tenant's security deposit from the tenant's rent without necessity of lawsuit or obtain a refund of the tenant's security deposit pursuant to law;

(5) if the lease is terminated by the tenant, recover a pro rata refund of any advance rentals paid from the date of termination or the date the tenant moves out, whichever is later;

(6) recover actual damages, including but not limited to moving costs, utility connection fees, storage fees, and lost wages from work; and

(7) recover court costs and attorney's fees, excluding any attorney's fees for a cause of action for damages relating to a personal injury.

(c) When deducting for the tenant's payment of the landlord's utility bill under this section, the tenant shall submit to the landlord a copy of a receipt from the utility company which evidences the amount of payment made by the tenant to reconnect or avert cutoff of utilities.

(d) The tenant remedies under this section are effective on the date the tenant has notice from the utility company of a future cutoff or notice of an actual cutoff, whichever is sooner. However, the tenant's remedies under this section shall cease if:

(1) the landlord provides the tenant with written evidence from the utility that all delinquent sums due the utility have been paid in full; and

145

(2) at the time the tenant receives such evidence, the tenant has not yet terminated the lease or filed suit under this section.

§ 92.302 Notice of Utility Disconnection of Nonsubmetered Master Metered Multifamily Property to Municipalities, Owners, and Tenants

(a) In this section:

(1) "Customer" means a person who is responsible for bills received for electric utility service or gas utility service provided to nonsubmetered master metered multifamily property.

(2) "Nonsubmetered master metered multifamily property" means an apartment, a leased or owner-occupied condominium, or one or more buildings containing at least 10 dwellings that receive electric utility service or gas utility service that is master metered but not submetered.

(b) A customer shall provide written notice of a service disconnection to each tenant or owner at a nonsubmetered master metered multifamily property not later than the fifth day after the date the customer receives a notice of service disconnection from an electric service provider or a gas utility. The customer must provide the notice by mail to the tenant's or owner's preferred mailing address or hand deliver the notice to the tenant or owner. The written notice must include the customer's contact information and the tenant's remedies under § 92.301. The notice must include the following text in both English and Spanish:

"Notice to residents of (name and address of nonsubmetered master metered multifamily property): Electric (or gas) service to this property is scheduled for disconnection on (date) because (reason for disconnection)."

(c) If the property is located in a municipality, the customer shall provide the same notice described by Subsection (b) to the governing body of that municipality by certified mail. The governing body of the municipality may provide additional notice to the property's tenants and owners after receipt of the service disconnection notice under this subsection.

(d) A customer is not required to provide the notices described by this section if the customer avoids the disconnection by paying the bill.

SUBCHAPTER H. RETALIATION

§ 92.331 Retaliation by landlord
   (a) A landlord may not retaliate against a tenant by taking an action described by Subsection (b) because the tenant:
   (1) in good faith exercises or attempts to exercise against a landlord a right or remedy granted to the tenant by lease, municipal ordinance, or federal or state statute;
   (2) gives a landlord a notice to repair or exercise a remedy under this chapter;
   (3) complains to a governmental entity responsible for enforcing building or housing codes, a public utility, or a civic or nonprofit agency, and the tenant:
      (A) claims a building or housing code violation or utility problem; and
      (B) believes in good faith that the complaint is valid and that the violation or problem occurred; or
   (4) establishes, attempts to establish, or participates in a tenant organization.
   (b) A landlord may not, within six months after the date of the tenant's action under Subsection (a), retaliate against the tenant by:
   (1) filing an eviction proceeding, except for the grounds stated by § 92.332;
   (2) depriving the tenant of the use of the premises, except for reasons authorized by law;
   (3) decreasing services to the tenant;
   (4) increasing the tenant's rent or terminating the tenant's lease; or
   (5) engaging, in bad faith, in a course of conduct that materially interferes with the tenant's rights under the tenant's lease.

§ 92.332 Nonretaliation
   (a) The landlord is not liable for retaliation under this subchapter if the landlord proves that the action was not made for purposes of retaliation, nor is the landlord liable, unless the action violates a prior court order under § 92.0563, for:
   (1) increasing rent under an escalation clause in a written lease for utilities, taxes, or insurance; or

(2) increasing rent or reducing services as part of a pattern of rent increases or service reductions for an entire multidwelling project.

(b) An eviction or lease termination based on the following circumstances, which are valid grounds for eviction or lease termination in any event, does not constitute retaliation:

(1) the tenant is delinquent in rent when the landlord gives notice to vacate or files an eviction action;

(2) the tenant, a member of the tenant's family, or a guest or invitee of the tenant intentionally damages property on the premises or by word or conduct threatens the personal safety of the landlord, the landlord's employees, or another tenant;

(3) the tenant has materially breached the lease, other than by holding over, by an action such as violating written lease provisions prohibiting serious misconduct or criminal acts, except as provided by this section;

(4) the tenant holds over after giving notice of termination or intent to vacate;

(5) the tenant holds over after the landlord gives notice of termination at the end of the rental term and the tenant does not take action under § 92.331 until after the landlord gives notice of termination; or

(6) the tenant holds over and the landlord's notice of termination is motivated by a good faith belief that the tenant, a member of the tenant's family, or a guest or invitee of the tenant might:

(A) adversely affect the quiet enjoyment by other tenants or neighbors;

(B) materially affect the health or safety of the landlord, other tenants, or neighbors; or

(C) damage the property of the landlord, other tenants, or neighbors.

§ 92.333 Tenant Remedies

In addition to other remedies provided by law, if a landlord retaliates against a tenant under this subchapter, the tenant may recover from the landlord a civil penalty of one month's rent plus $500, actual damages, court costs, and reasonable attorney's fees in an action for recovery of property damages, moving costs, actual expenses, civil penalties, or declaratory or injunctive relief, less any delinquent rents or other sums for which the tenant is liable to the landlord. If the tenant's rent payment to the landlord is subsidized in whole or in part by a governmental entity, the civil penalty granted under this section shall reflect the fair market rent of the dwelling plus $500.

§ 92.334 Invalid Complaints

(a) If a tenant files or prosecutes a suit for retaliatory action based on a complaint asserted under § 92.331(a)(3), and the government building or housing inspector or utility company representative visits the premises and determines in writing that a violation of a building or housing code does not exist or that a utility problem does not exist, there is a rebuttable presumption that the tenant acted in bad faith.

(b) If a tenant files or prosecutes a suit under this subchapter in bad faith, the landlord may recover possession of the dwelling unit and may recover from the tenant a civil penalty of one month's rent plus $500, court costs, and reasonable attorney's fees.   If the tenant's rent payment to the landlord is subsidized in whole or in part by a governmental entity, the civil penalty granted under this section shall reflect the fair market rent of the dwelling plus $500.

§ 92.335 Eviction Suits

In an eviction suit, retaliation by the landlord under § 92.331 is a defense and a rent deduction lawfully made by the tenant under this chapter is a defense for nonpayment of the rent to the extent allowed by this chapter. Other judicial actions under this chapter may not be joined with an eviction suit or asserted as a defense or crossclaim in an eviction suit.

SUBCHAPTER I. RENTAL APPLICATION

§ 92.351 Definitions
For purposes of this subchapter:
(1) "Application deposit" means a sum of money that is given to the landlord in connection with a rental application and that is refundable to the applicant if the applicant is rejected as a tenant.
(1-a) "Application fee" means a nonrefundable sum of money that is given to the landlord to offset the costs of screening an applicant for acceptance as a tenant.
(2) "Applicant" or "rental applicant" means a person who makes an application to a landlord for rental of a dwelling.
(3) "Co-applicant" means a person who makes an application for rental of a dwelling with other applicants and who plans to live in the dwelling with other applicants.
(4) "Deposited" means deposited in an account of the landlord or the landlord's agent in a bank or other financial institution.
(5) "Landlord" means a prospective landlord to whom a person makes application for rental of a dwelling.
(5-a) "Rental application" means a written request made by an applicant to a landlord to lease premises from the landlord.
(6) "Required date" means the required date for any acceptance of the applicant under § 92.352.

§ 92.3515 Notice of Eligibility Requirements
(a) At the time an applicant is provided with a rental application, the landlord shall make available to the applicant printed notice of the landlord's tenant selection criteria and the grounds for which the rental application may be denied, including the applicant's:
(1) criminal history;
(2) previous rental history;
(3) current income;
(4) credit history; or
(5) failure to provide accurate or complete information on the application form.
(b) If the landlord makes the notice available under Subsection (a), the applicant shall sign an acknowledgment indicating the notice was made

available. If the acknowledgment is not signed, there is a rebuttable presumption that the notice was not made available to the applicant.

(c) The acknowledgment required by Subsection (b) must include a statement substantively equivalent to the following: "Signing this acknowledgment indicates that you have had the opportunity to review the landlord's tenant selection criteria.   The tenant selection criteria may include factors such as criminal history, credit history, current income, and rental history. If you do not meet the selection criteria, or if you provide inaccurate or incomplete information, your application may be rejected and your application fee will not be refunded."

(d) The acknowledgment may be part of the rental application if the notice is underlined or in bold print.

(e) If the landlord rejects an applicant and the landlord has not made the notice required by Subsection (a) available, the landlord shall return the application fee and any application deposit.

(f) If an applicant requests a landlord to mail a refund of the applicant's application fee to the applicant, the landlord shall mail the refund check to the applicant at the address furnished by the applicant.

§ 92.352 Rejection of Applicant

(a) The applicant is deemed rejected by the landlord if the landlord does not give notice of acceptance of the applicant on or before the seventh day after the:

(1) date the applicant submits a completed rental application to the landlord on an application form furnished by the landlord; or

(2) date the landlord accepts an application deposit if the landlord does not furnish the applicant an application form.

(b) A landlord's rejection of one co-applicant shall be deemed as a rejection of all co-applicants.

§ 92.353   Procedures for Notice or Refund

(a) Except as provided in Subsection (b), a landlord is presumed to have given notice of an applicant's acceptance or rejection if the notice is by:

(1) telephone to the applicant, co-applicant, or a person living with the applicant or co-applicant on or before the required date; or

(2) United States mail, addressed to the applicant and postmarked on or before the required date.

(b) If a rental applicant requests that any acceptance of the applicant or any refund of the applicant's application deposit be mailed to the applicant, the landlord must mail the refund check to the applicant at the address furnished by the applicant.

(c) If the date of required notice of acceptance or required refund of an application deposit is a Saturday, Sunday, or state or federal holiday, the required date shall be extended to the end of the next day following the Saturday, Sunday, or holiday.

§ 92.354 Liability of Landlord

A landlord who in bad faith fails to refund an application fee or deposit in violation of this subchapter is liable for an amount equal to the sum of $100, three times the amount wrongfully retained, and the applicant's reasonable attorney's fees.

Made in the USA
Coppell, TX
16 June 2025